Thicket P.....y
Rebirth and the Return of the Nuns

Colin Blanshard Withers

2022

Preface

Thicket Priory I was founded before 1180, possibly as early as 1162, as a Benedictine priory of nuns which survived until it was dissolved by Henry VIII in 1539. The story of the priory from Foundation to Dissolution has been related in the first booklet in this series and covers the period from 1162 to 1539.

The site of the priory then fell into decay but Thicket Priory II was eventually built adjacent to the site of the original in the middle to late seventeenth century. The story from Dissolution to Thicket Priory II, which covers the period from 1539 to 1844, is told in the second booklet in the series and charts the ownership of the site until Thicket Priory II was built.

In this third booklet, the story of Thicket continues with the building of Thicket Priory III in 1844, which was designed by the celebrated architect Edward Blore, who worked on the designs of Buckingham Palace and many other famous buildings in England and abroad. The story continues through to the eventual sale in 1954 of Thicket Priory III by its private owners to Carmelite nuns who, after an interval of over four centuries, made Thicket Priory III a religious home for nuns once again. The story continues with their move to a more practical Thicket Priory IV, adjacent to Thicket Priory III, which once again was in lay hands.

Bishop's Stortford, October, 2022

Acknowledgements

My grateful thanks are due to the archivists and staff of The National Archives (TNA), who have been unstinting in their support and suggestions. My thanks are also due to Bruce Westcott and Dr. Matthew Tompkins of Leicester University for their help with the more tricky idiosyncrasies of medieval Latin and administrative practice. Thanks are also due to the staff of the Borthwick Institute for Archives at the University of York, for their help with the medieval registers of the archbishops of York; the staff of the Department of Manuscripts in the British Library; and all the staff of the various archives and libraries throughout Yorkshire who helped in locating and providing digital copies of many unpublished manuscripts.

My thanks must also go to the last remaining member of the Dunnington-Jefferson family who once lived at Thicket Priory, Rosemary Nicolette Dunnington-Jefferson (Nicky to her friends), who proof-read the entire text and provided many corrections and observations.

Last, but not least, my thanks are due to Bruce Corrie, the current owner of the reborn Thicket Priory whose support has been most encouraging.

Contents

Abbreviations

ACAD   A Cambridge Alumni Database (see Online Resources)

BI   The Borthwick Institute for Archives, University of York

BNA   The British Newspaper Archive (see Online Resources)

CP   The Complete Peerage

ERRO   East Riding Record Office, Beverley

HHC   Hull History Centre

HMSO   His/Her Majesty's Stationery Office

TNA   The National Archives, Kew, London

VCH   Victoria County History

YAS   Yorkshire Archaeological Society (Archives now held at the Brotherton Library, University of Leeds)

Bibliography and other Sources

All works producing two or more references in the text are included here. Works that produce a single reference in the text are quoted directly in the footnotes.

I. *Modern Works*

Chetham Society CHETHAM SOCIETY, Publications of, (Old, New and Third Series: many volumes, ongoing)

O'Neill O'NEILL, H. C., *The Royal Fusiliers in the Great War*, (London, 1922)

Pevsner, Neave PEVSNER, Nikolaus, NEAVE, David, *The Buildings of England, Yorkshire: York and the East Riding*, (2nd Edition, 1995)

Ruvigny RUVIGNY, The Marquis de, *The Roll of Honour, A biographical record of all members of His Majesty's naval and military forces who have fallen in the war*, vol. 1, (London, preface dated 1916)

Venn VENN, John Archibald, *Alumni Cantabrigienses; a biographical list of all known students, graduates and holders of office at the University of Cambridge, from the earliest times to 1900*, in 6 volumes, (Cambridge, 1940–1954)

VCH, *East* ALLISON, K. J., (ed.), A History of the County of York, East Riding: vol. 3, Ouse and Derwent Wapentake, and Part of Harthill Wapentake, (London, 1976)

Ward WARD, J. T., *East Yorkshire Landed Estates in the Nineteenth Century*, East Yorkshire Local History Society Series, n. 23 (1967)

| Withers, *Foundation to Dissolution* | WITHERS, Colin B., *Thicket Priory: Foundation to Dissolution*, (Amazon:Booklet and Kindle e-Book, 2022) |
| Withers, *Dissolution to Thicket Priory II* | WITHERS, Colin B., *Thicket Priory: Dissolution to Thicket Priory II*, (Amazon: Booklet and Kindle e-Book, 2022) |

II. Unprinted Public Records and Manuscripts

The National Archives

PROB 11   Prerogative Court of Canterbury Wills

Borthwick Institute for Archives, University of York

Dirge   *A Munition Dirge*, Cooke, Troughton and Simms Archives
PR THORG   Parish Registers of Thorganby
YWT/5/52/1/3/3 Purchase of Thicket Priory

British Library

Add MS 42028   fols. 98–100, Designs for Thicket Priory
Add MS 42029   fols. 71–72, 100, Designs for Thicket Priory
Add MS 42043   fol. 20, Designs for Thicket Priory
Add MS 47610   Edward Blore's plans of Thicket Priory
Lansd, MS 914   Samuel Buck's Yorkshire Sketchbook

East Riding Archives

DDX225/12   Particulars of sale relating to Thicket Priory Estate
DDX683/11   Parliamentary survey
DDMT/627   Copy Wills Book, 1794–1851
DDMT/628   Copy Wills Book, 1759–1907
DDMT/629   Copy Wills Book, 1807–1890
JL/7/1990/1   History of Thorganby in 1908

Hull History Centre

U DDJ   Papers of the Dunnington-Jefferson Family of Thicket

III. Online Resources

A Cambridge Alumni Database	http://venn.lib.cam.ac.uk/
British Newspaper Archive	https://www.britishnewspaperarchive.co.uk/ (£charge)
Find A Will	England & Wales Government Probate Death Index, https://probatesearch.service.gov.uk/#wills (£charge)
Find My Past	https://www.findmypast.com/ (£charge)

CHAPTER 1

Thorganby Hall and Thicket Priory III
John Dunnington-Jefferson 1 – Thorganby Hall – Joseph Dunnington-Jefferson junior – Coat of Arms – The Building of Thicket Priory III

In compliance with the will of Robert Jefferson discussed in Booklet 2 in the series, John Dunnington applied for a Royal Licence to add the name 'Jefferson' to his own. The licence was granted 29 January 1812 and was published in *The London Gazette*.[1]

In 1822 John Dunnington-Jefferson rebuilt Thorganby Hall. The original Thorganby Hall was probably the 'Hall House' sold in 1802 by Thomas Bradford to John Dunnington. The hall still stands to this day, with the arms of the Dunnington family engraved in stone high above the entrance door with the date 1882 below the arms.

John Dunnington-Jefferson of Thorganby Hall died in 1840 and was buried 22 September at Thorganby.[2] He had made a will, probated at the Prerogative Court of York, with an estate valued at £35,000, an enormous sum in those days, and worth over three million pounds by today's standards.[3] His brother and sister, Thomas and Jane, continued to live at Thorganby Hall.[4]

The estate was inherited by John's nephew, Joseph Dunnington *junior*, son of John's brother, Joseph Dunnington *senior* who had married Mary Toutill in 1805.[5]

---

[1] BNA, *The London Gazette*, 1 February 1812, Issue 16570, p. 226

[2] BI, Ref: PR–THORG–6, p. 25

[3] BI, Ref: Prob. Reg. 202, fol. 403. The value of the estate in today's terms was estimated using the Calculator at: https://www.measuringworth.com/calculators/ppoweruk/. A transcript of the will can be found in the Appendix: Family Wills

[4] TNA, 1841 Census: Ref: HO 107–1228, Book 16, fol.3, p. 1

[5] Joseph Dunnington was born 17 July 1807, and baptised two days later at Thorganby. BI, Ref: PR THORG/8. His father and mother, Joseph Dunnington and Mary Toutill, were married by licence at Birkin, his mother's home parish, 3 December 1805. BI, Refs: Archbishop of York's Marriage Licence Allegations; Birkin, Bishops' Transcripts of Marriages

Joseph Dunnington *junior* went to school in Manchester[6] and went on to attend St John's, Cambridge, in 1825, gaining his BA in 1830 and his MA in 1833. He was ordained deacon in 1831 and priest in 1832, becoming vicar of Thorganby the same year.[7]

Joseph *junior* married Anna Mervynia Vavasour, eldest daughter of Lieutenant General Sir Henry Maghull Mervin Vavasour, 2nd Bart. of the Horse Grenadier Guards, by Anne Vavasour, eldest daughter of William Vavasour of Dublin, LLD, by licence at Monkstown near Dublin, 23 May 1839.[8] Sir Henry had died in 1838, and Anna was probably with her recently widowed mother in Dublin, possibly explaining why she and Joseph had married in the nearby affluent suburb of Monkstown.

Following the return to Thicket Priory, the Rev. Joseph obtained a licence from the Archbishop of York in 1839 to settle his ecclesiastical residence at Thicket Priory, instead of the usual curate's house, as the curate's house was considered unfit for the Rev. Joseph's station in life.[9] The following year the happy couple had their first child, a daughter, Mervynia, who was baptised at Thorganby, 29 November 1840. [10]

Like his uncle, in order to inherit the estate, Joseph also underwent a change of name, assuming the surname of Jefferson by Royal Licence in 1841.[11]

> *Whitehall, May* 21, 1841.
>
> The Queen has been pleased to grant unto Joseph Dunnington, of Thicket Priory, in the county of York, Clerk, Master of Arts, Her Majesty's royal licence and authority, that he and his issue may, out of grateful respect for the memory of Robert

---

[6] Chetham Society, vol. 94, Chetham Miscellanies, The Admission Register of the Manchester School, (1874), p. 183

[7] ACAD

[8] Appendix to the Thirtieth Report of the Deputy Keeper of the Public Records…Ireland, 1899, Diocese of Dublin Act Books, p. 1069; *The Gentleman's Magazine*, vol. 166, p. 195

[9] HHC, Ref: DDJ/14/398

[10] BI, Ref: PR THORG/4, p. 37. 1841 Census: Ref: HO 107–1228, Book 16, fol.7, p. 9

[11] BNA, *The London Gazette*, 21 May 1841, Issue 19980, p. 1282.

Jefferson, late of Howden, in the said county, Esq. deceased, take and henceforth use the surname of Jefferson, in addition to and after that of Dunnington, and also bear the arms of Jefferson quarterly, in the first quarter, with his own family arms; such arms being first duly exemplified according to the laws of arms, and recorded in the Heralds' Office, otherwise the said royal licence and permission to be void and of none effect: And also to command, that the said royal concession and declaration be recorded in Her Majesty's College of Arms.

It is not clear from the above announcement whether the quartering of arms and their registration at the College of Arms was a condition of the granting of the Royal Licence to effect the change of name, or whether the application made by Joseph for a change of name also included a request for a coat of arms. As the announcement makes clear that the failure to exemplify the arms in the Heralds' Office would void the Royal Licence, it would appear that the former is the case.

Dunnington-Jefferson Arms

This exemplification of the Dunnington-Jefferson coat of arms shows the quartering. In the 1st and 4th quarters the arms of Jefferson are shown. The blazon[12] for this coat of arms is as follows: gu. a griffin sejant, wings endorsed ar. a border engr. of the last charge with eight pellets, for Jefferson. Translating the heraldic language into plain English, this means that the background colour of the shield is red (gu. = gules = red), and on

---

[12] A 'blazon' is a textual description of a coat of arms, written in heraldic language

that background is a griffin sitting on its haunches (sejant) with its wings spread upwards (wings endorsed), and coloured white (ar. = argent = silver, normally depicted as white) and the shield having a border all around it with small semi-circular indents (engr. = engrailed), also coloured white (of the last—means of the last colour mentioned), with eight small black dots (pellets) spaced around the border.

In the 2nd and 3rd quarters the arms of Dunnington are shown. The blazon for this coat of arms is as follows: paly of six ar. and az. on a chief gu. a bezant between two annulets or, for Dunnington. In plain English this means that the shield is divided into six vertical bars of equal width (paly of six), with the first being coloured white (ar. = argent = silver = white), and the next coloured blue (az. = azure = blue), alternatively. The shield is then divided again, having a separate top area (chief) coloured red (gu. = gules = red), with a bezant (a gold coin, common in the Holy Land during the Crusades), depicted as a solid yellow disc), between two rings of yellow (annulets).

I cannot find any reference to a member of either of the East Riding Jefferson or Dunnington families ever having been granted a coat of arms prior to this registration in the Heralds' College, and I suspect that these two coats, quartered, were designed by the College, rather than by the family. Some aspects of the coats are discernable though. The Dunnington coat of arms is very similar to the arms of the Donnington family (from a completely unrelated village of that name, and nothing to do with the village of Dunnington, just east of York where 'our' Dunnington family hails from). The arms have been 'differenced' slightly in that the arms of the Donnington family have three bezants in chief, whereas the arms of the Dunnington family have had two of these bezants turned into rings.

A pub sign for the Donnington Arms, near Oxford

In 1844 the Rev. Joseph Dunnington-Jefferson decided to have a new grand residence built, to replace the old Thicket Priory (Thicket Hall) of the Robinson family and embarked on an ambitious building project—a new Thicket Priory. The architect he employed for this prestigious project was none other than Edward Blore, notable for his works on Lambeth Palace,

Buckingham Palace, Hampton Court Palace, Windsor Castle, and many others.[13]

The Clerk of the Works for the building of Thicket Priory, Elliott Walter, kept meticulous accounts, but the bland numbers in the account books still revealed some interesting insights.[14]

The on-site work began at the end of May 1844. The men initially employed consisted of bricklayers, carpenters and labourers, but were joined by wood sawyers from the middle of June. The team of men was joined in early July by masons and stone sawyers, showing that the stonework was not cut and dressed off-site but rather on-site. In mid-July they were joined by a blacksmith, and in mid-August by brickmakers.

Some of the materials for the site arrived by river, particularly bricks and sand from Hull, via the Humber and lower reaches of the Derwent, and Malton stone from the upper reaches of the Derwent. The accounts recorded many payments for 'river dues'.

Blore came to Thicket twice before the on-site work began, on 13th October 1843, and 10th March 1844. He followed this up with journeys for meetings on 16th June, 2nd July and 2nd September through 1844.

The on-site workmen continued apace during 1845, and were eventually joined by plumbers and slaters in the May and plasterers in the August. From 18th April to 17th October a Mr. Robert Dryden appears on the payroll, who had been hired as foreman of the Clerk of the Works.

In 1847 we learn that Robert Dryden has taken over as the Clerk of the Works, though receiving 50s. per week as opposed to the 63s. per week received by his predecessor, Elliott Walter.

By the end of 1847 the work was essentially complete. The only work listed during 1848 was for the fitting of the chapel, and designs for new lodges. Blore made his last visit to Thicket on 17th April. The cost for building the new Thicket Priory was close to £20,000.

While the work on building the new Thicket Priory was going on, a terrible accident occurred. A newspaper of the day reported it thus:

---

[13] Edward Blore's major works are listed here:
en.wikipedia.org/wiki/List_of_works_by_Edward_Blore_on_palaces_and_large_houses
[14] HHC, Refs: U DDJ/34/105–8

MELANCHOLY AND FATAL OCCURRENCE. --- An event in strict accordance with this heading occurred on Monday week, at the beautiful mansion which is now in the course of erection by the Rev. J. D. Jefferson, at Thicket Priory, in the East Riding of this county. On the morning of that day a promising young man named Benjamin Buckley, a bricklayer, was engaged at work on the top of the building, when owing to some unaccountable mishap his foot slipped, and he was precipitated to the foundation of the structure, a distance of 192 feet, and almost dashed to pieces. The unfortunate youth was taken up in a state of insensibility; but by medical assistance and proper nourishment he continued to breathe until the subsequent Wednesday, when death put a period to his sufferings. An inquest was held on Thursday at the County Hospital, in Wheldrake, before John Wood, Esq., the coroner, and a respectable jury, when a verdict of 'accidental death' was returned. The deceased was a native of this town, and, what adds to the melancholy circumstance, was to have been married to a respectable young female at Wheldrake on the day on which his remains were consigned to the tomb.[15]

During the construction of Thicket Priory, the Reverend Joseph also laid plans in 1846 for the rebuilding of Ellerton Priory,[16] paying £695 to Simpson and Malone, stonemasons and carpenters of Hull, to carry out the work. The beautiful little church was completed and consecrated 26 April 1848 by the Archbishop of York.[17]

Mention has been made of the birth of Mervynia, the daughter of Joseph and Anna, in 1840. The couple went on to have a further eight children: Caroline Emma, bap. 23 October 1842; Mary Campbell, bap. 1 December 1844; Joseph John, bap. 21 December 1845; Henry Mervyn and Thomas, twin boys, bap. 22 January 1847; Theodosia, bap. 30 July 1848; Mervyn, bap. 31 March 1850; and Thomas Trafford, bap. 3 April 1853. Unfortunately, tragedy struck the family, with the twin boys, Henry Mervyn and Thomas, dying as newborns, and they were buried together, 27 January 1847, just five days after their baptism; and Caroline Emma, dying at the age of ten in a terrible accident at Scarborough, when she fell over the balustrades in the guest house where she was staying and was killed instantly.

---

[15] BNA, *Bradford Observer* 2 Oct 1845, p.5, col. 4. The County Hospital was a public house
[16] HHC, Refs: U DDJ/6/3–7
[17] BNA, *York Herald*, 19 Apr 1848

Thicket Priory III

CHAPTER 2
Victorian Life at the Priory
Reverend Joseph Dunnington-Jefferson – Mervyn Dunnington-Jefferson – Joseph John Dunnington-Jefferson

The Reverend Joseph was an archetypal country gentleman. He was the perpetual curate of Thorganby, a canon of York Minster, a local magistrate, and the lord of several manors, including Thorganby, West Cottingwith, Bellasize, Eastrington, Gilberdyke, Harlethorpe, Newport and Goole. Along with Thicket Priory and its 150-acre park he controlled 7,278 acres in the East Riding, producing an annual rental of £10,936, along with 533 acres in the West Riding, worth another £1,067.[18] He also chaired many local charities and local action groups. As well as supporting the school in West Cottingwith, (originally set up by Thomas Dunnington in 1733), the Reverend also erected a free school and chapel in Newport which opened on 18 April 1855,[19] and was heavily involved in the erection of the new church in Fulford which opened in December 1866.[20]

The Reverend's big passions were cattle breeding, amassing many awards for his shorthorn cattle, and breeding pedigree horses which he bred at his Thicket Priory Stud Farm.[21] He was also a member of the Royal Agricultural Society of England,[22] and an active country sportsman, hosting many shoots, as well as fox-hunting and fishing expeditions.

To maintain his hunting rights on his estates, the Reverend employed several local men as gamekeepers, and unfortunately a nasty accident befell

---

[18] Ward, p. 43. The acreage and rental yield were those enumerated in the *Return of Owners of Land, 1873, vol. II, Northampton to York.* Unfortunately there are no known surviving manorial documents for any of the manors that the Dunnington-Jefferson family held

[19] Newport is on the B1230 road, one mile east of Gilberdyke, close to Scalby. The opening of the chapel and school was reported in the *Goole and Marshland Gazette* edition of April 1855

[20] HHC: Letter Books, Ref: U DDJ-40-10 part 1, 1 March 1832–31 March 1864. Letters dated 19 Apr 1865 and 12 Feb 1864, respectively, and *passim*

[21] The local newspapers carried numerous reports of agricultural shows featuring the animals from the Thicket Priory Stud Farm and the awards they won, throughout the Victorian period

[22] BNA, *Bell's Weekly Messenger* newspaper, dated 5 June 1843, carried his election

one of them. A Mr. Jacques, one of the Reverend's gamekeepers, was out shooting rabbits with his son, when the son accidently shot his father, the said Mr. Jacques, and 15 pieces of buckshot lodged in his shoulder. A newspaper of the day reported the accident and went on to say that Mr. Jacques was now 'in a very precarious state'.[23]

Both the Reverend Joseph and his son Mervyn played cricket,[24] and the Thicket Priory cricket team hosted numerous local sides at Thicket, winning more matches than they lost. Mervyn was a member of the York Cricket Club, for which his father paid 1 guinea annually for his membership.[25] Thicket also had a football team, and 'The Priors' played football in the Derwent League.[26] The priory also hosted several local angling groups to fish the Derwent from the priory grounds and many prize fish were caught there.[27] The family was very active in the social scene of the Victorian period, attending many functions and charity events, and frequently organised fêtes at the priory for schools, workhouse children, and the elderly.

The Reverend's many pursuits, plus his charitable projects and his official duties in the county, meant that he could devote very little time to his local pastoral care. To remedy this situation he began a search for a curate to take on these duties at Thorganby church.

---

[23] BNA, *Hull Packet*, 24 Apr 1846

[24] BNA, *The Sportsman*, 1 September 1869. This newspaper article shows them both playing against Fulford, which Thicket lost by 20 runs. Unfortunately the Reverend was out for 3, caught by Lindley, bowled Clarke, while Mervyn was out for a duck, st. Marshall, bowled Clarke

[25] HHC: Letter-Books, Ref: U DDJ-40-10 part 1, 1 March 1832–31 March 1864. Letter dated 23 Mar 1864. In1869 Mervyn was now a member of the Yorkshire Gentlemen's Cricket Club, with his father again paying 1 guinea for the annual subscription. Letter dated 20 May 1869

[26] The local newspapers also carried weekly home and away reports of cricket or football, depending on the season, involving Thicket Priory, e.g.: BNA, *Yorkshire Gazette*, 18 Aug 1888, p. 8 col. 1; *Yorkshire Gazette*, 7 Jan 1899, p. 2 cols. 1–2; *Hull Daily Mail*, 10 Oct 1922, p. 4 col. 4

[27] For example: *York Herald*, 21 September, 1889, p. 13, col. 1

Letters were sent out throughout 1864,[28] and eventually a suitable candidate was found, in the person of the Rev. Joseph Thomlinson.[29]

With so many responsibilities on his shoulders time was of the essence to the Reverend. He even wrote a letter to the Secretary of the General Post Office in London complaining about the time that letters were normally delivered to Thicket Priory, generally about 10.30am, leaving him with no time to reply by the same post. He requested that the route for deliveries of letters in this area of the East Riding be rearranged so that he could receive his letters earlier. It is not known if this request was granted.[30]

The family was very well thought of in the area, due in no small part to the frequent charitable events held at Thicket—teas and outings for the orphans and schoolchildren of the locale, and the occasional generous gestures to their many tenants, such as was reported in the newspapers of March 1850:

> We have the pleasure of informing our readers that the Rev. J. D. Jefferson, of Thicket Priory, at his recent rent day, at the house of Mr. Bowman, the Commercial Inn, Howden, made a proposal to his numerous tenantry, either to return them ten per cent. on their half-year's rent, or allow them twenty per cent. in tillage.[31]

The 1851 census tells us which family members were residing at Thicket Priory and also provides a snapshot of the household servants.[32] The family included: Joseph Dunnington-Jefferson, head, 43, and is described as magistrate and perpetual curate at Thorganby; Anna Mervynia, wife, 38; and their children, Mervynia Jane, 10; Caroline Emma, 8; Mary Campbell, 6; Joseph John, 5; Theodosia, 2; and Mervyn, 1. The 12 servants were listed next, first the upstairs staff: Sarah Walmsley, 35, governess, of Tynemouth; Thomas Strickland, 31, footman, of Edstone, Yorks; Robert Gibbon, 25, coachman, of Whorlton, co. Durham; and John White, 16, page.

---

[28] HHC: Letter-Books, Ref: U DDJ-40-10 part 1, 1 March 1832–31 March 1864. Letters dated 10 Feb 1864, 15 Feb 1864, 22 Mar 1864

[29] HHC: HH 26 May 1865. Clergy List for 1866, p. 334

[30] HHC: Letter-Books, Ref: U DDJ-40-10 part 1, 1 March 1832–31 March 1864. Letter dated 29 Mar 1864

[31] BNA, *Yorkshire Gazette,* 16 Mar 1850

[32] TNA, Ref: HO 1072356, fol. 75, p. 19

The downstairs staff included: Elizabeth Balmborough, 58, housekeeper, of Yorkshire; Eliza Lascelles Cowburn, 42, nurse, of Bishopwearmouth; Jane Barton, 33, housemaid, of Acomb; Mary Kettlewell, 22, dairy maid, of Tadcaster; Mary Todd, 18, kitchen maid, of Askham Bryan; Ann Allison, 18, housemaid, of Thorganby; Anna Fletcher, 17, nursery maid, of York; and Mary Newsome, 61, labourer's wife, of Aughton. The other member of the family in the area, the Reverend Joseph's aunt, Jane Dunnington, 83, was living at nearby Thorganby Hall, accompanied by four servants: a cook and housemaid (combined); a dairy maid; a coachman; and errand boy. It is noticeable that there was no Thicket Lodge mentioned on the 1851 census, but it does appear from the census of 1861 onwards.

The Thicket Priory Estate was expanded again in 1858, when the Newbald Hall Estate was broken up and sold in lots at auction.[33] The Reverend bought Bullens Hill Farm, of just over 254 acres for £12,700, and Sober-Hill Farm, of just over 477 acres for £19,000.

The 1861 census shows that the family had sadly lost a daughter, Caroline Emma, in the intervening ten years, but had gained a son, Thomas Trafford. Caroline Emma had died in a terrible accident at Scarborough as mentioned in the previous chapter. Also on the census we learn that the servants were now supplemented by a lady's maid, a groom and an assistant laundry maid. Thicket Priory Lodge was now mentioned for the first time, where William Rogers resided with his wife and son, and where William, in addition to being the gatekeeper of Thicket Priory, was also employed as a gardener.[34] Jane Dunnington was still going strong at Thorganby, and now aged 92, accompanied by her four servants.[35]

Joseph is absent on the 1871 census, but his son Joseph John was there with his wife, Emma, showing she was aged 20, and had been born in Ireland. The house had a full complement of 10 servants, and Thicket Lodge was now occupied by William Smith and his family.[36]

---

[33] The Newbald Hall Estate had been with the Clough family of bankers. The head, John Clough Esq., had located his seat at Clifton House, near York, while his son, William Clough, resided at Newbald Hall during the selling of the estate lands there

[34] TNA, Ref: RG 09/3555, fol. 53, p. 1

[35] TNA, Ref: RG 09/3555, fol. 61, p. 17

[36] TNA, Ref: RG 10/4754, fol. 56, p. 1

Aunt Jane Dunnington of Thorganby Hall had died before this census year and was buried at Thorganby, 26 March 1863; the hall was then leased to Charles Tunnard and his family.[37]

The 1870s were to bring much joy to the Dunnington-Jefferson family, with two marriages to celebrate. First was of the eldest son, Joseph John, who married Emma Sarah Stoney, the second daughter of Mr. T. B. Stoney, JP, of Portland Park, Tipperary. The marriage took place in the village of Lorrah, Co. Down. The bridegroom was attended by the Count de Bros as his best man, with several army officers as groomsmen. The bride was attended by the three sisters of the groom, Mervynia, Mary Campbell and Theodosia, plus several other ladies. The ceremony was performed by the Venerable Archdeacon Knox, and afterwards a *déjeuner* was served to upwards of eighty guests under a marquee in Portland Park. After the celebrations the bride and groom left by special train for Dublin, en route to Wales.[38]

Six years later it was the turn of Joseph John's sister to get married, Mary Campbell Dunnington-Jefferson. This was a less grand affair than that of the eldest son, and unusually did not take place in the home parish of the bride. The marriage ceremony was performed in the parish church of Saints Peter and Paul, Wadhurst, Sussex, where the groom had previously been curate. The groom was the Rev. Frederick Field-Richards, English Chaplain at Toulon,[39] the eldest son of Frederick Richards, The Briars, Hastings. They had one child, John Charles Field-Richards, who was a motorboat racing double gold medal winner in the 1908 Olympics. Mary's husband, Frederick, died in April 1879, and was buried in Hastings.[40]

Back at Thicket, in the September of 1879, the lady of the house, Anna Mervynia, was advertising for a curate for Thorganby, to have sole charge,

---

[37] TNA, Ref: RG 10/4754, fol. 60, p. 9

[38] BNA, *Richmond & Ripon Chronicle*, 1 Oct 1870. The marriage was fully described in this newspaper article

[39] Toulon was the French equivalent of Portsmouth. It was a large shipbuilding, ship repair yard and ship provisioning station, open to all ships (except in times of war), and was regularly used by British ships for repairs or re-provisioning

[40] In 1881 Mary remarried, in Hastings, William Robert White MD. Mary Campbell was the only one of the four sisters to marry. Caroline Emma had died young in a terrible accident already referred to, and Mervynia and Theodosia both later died unmarried

starting in the October, with a salary of £150 per annum, and to include a house. Her husband, the Rev. Joseph Dunnington-Jefferson was the perpetual curate at Thorganby, but was now in his seventies and possibly the curacy was getting too much for him.

The Reverend Joseph died 31 July 1880 and was buried a week later at Thorganby the following 6 August, aged 73.[41] His obituary appeared in all the national and provincial newspapers of the day. The Reverend's youngest son, Thomas Trafford Dunnington-Jefferson, died the year after his father, at the relatively young age of 29, and was buried at Thorganby 4 April 1882.[42]

The 1881 census reveals that at Thicket only one member of the family was in residence, Mervynia Jane, her age being given as 40 years, and her status as 'daughter of the head of household'. She was accompanied by nine servants: Sarah Steele, the cook and housekeeper; Emily Roxby, sewing maid; Mary Chaplin, housemaid; Anne Wallsington, laundry maid; Laura Hague, housemaid; Hannah Gibson, dairy maid; Sarah Smith, kitchen maid; George Ablet Hughes, footman; and Henry Davice, groom. Missing was the butler, who we know was Frederick Henry Babs in 1882.[43]

The eldest son, Joseph John Dunnington-Jefferson, was educated at Eton and was admitted a pensioner at Trinity College, Cambridge in 1863, matriculating in 1864, and gaining his BA in 1868, and his MA in 1871. He was admitted into the Inner Temple in February 1868, and called to the bar in May 1871. He joined the Yorkshire Hussars, rising from sub-lieutenant to lieutenant in 1876, to captain in 1883.[44]

Joseph John was appointed deputy lieutenant of the East Riding of the County of York, and the Borough of Kingston-upon-Hull in February 1884.

---

[41] BI, Ref: PR THORG/6, p. 58

[42] BI, Ref: PR THORG/6, p. 60

[43] Frederick describes himself as butler, of Thicket Priory, when he witnessed a lease involving Joseph John Dunnington-Jefferson, one of the trustees of the Hook and Goole Charity. ERRO, Ref: DDX2009/1/5/7/10

[44] ACAD: http://venn.lib.cam.ac.uk/cgi-bin/search-2018.pl?sur=Jefferson&suro=w&fir=Joseph&firo=c&cit=&cito=c&c=all&z=all&tex=&sye=&eye=&col=all&maxcount=50

He was selected as the Conservative Party candidate for the Morley Division in October 1885,[45] and like his father, he was also a magistrate for the county.

In May 1885, the London newspapers were announcing the arrival of members of the aristocracy and gentry for the 'season', and included the entry: 'Mr. and Mrs. Dunnington-Jefferson have arrived at 4 Wilton Street, from Thicket Priory',[46] indicating that they were very much into the Victorian societal scene at this time.

The second son of the Reverend Joseph, Mervyn Dunnington Jefferson, was born on 10 February 1850, and baptised at Thorganby 31 March 1850. He was educated at Eton and joined the 33rd Regiment of Foot in 1869 as an ensign, rising to lieutenant in 1871. Initially serving at home, he saw his first overseas service in September 1869 when he was in the East Indies until April 1878, followed by service in the Cape of Good Hope until November 1879. The following year he was promoted to captain and again saw service in the East Indies 13 March 1880–12 March 1881, returning to his home depot 13 March 1881.

The captain then took a leave of absence to get married, on 5 May 1881, at St. Michael le Belfrey in York, to Louisa Dorothy Barry, the daughter of the late Reverend John Barry, rector of Great Smeaton.[47] He retired from the army on half-pay 23 August 1881, and following a family tradition became a magistrate. Following his marriage, the captain and his wife led a somewhat peripatetic life. From at least March 1882 they were in the family's Wilton Street house in Belgravia, as their first child, Dorothy, was born there.[48]

---

[45] BNA, *Leeds Mercury*, 12 Oct 1885, p. 7. Joseph John lost to his Liberal Party opponent, Charles Milnes Gaskell, who polled 6,684 votes to Joseph John's 3,177

[46] Wilton Street is in Belgravia. It abuts Grosvenor Place, at the rear of the Buckingham Palace grounds, near Eaton Square. It resembles the house in the television drama, 'Upstairs Downstairs' set in Eaton Place

[47] BNA, *Yorkshire Gazette*, 14 May 1881, p. 3 column 6

[48] In the 1891 census Captain Mervyn gave the place of birth of his daughter Dorothy, now aged 9, as London, Wilton Street. TNA, Ref: RG12/1938, fol. 4, p. 2. This was the house owned by the captain's brother, Joseph John, and as March was well into the society 'season' it is not clear whether the captain and his wife were there for the season, or had been given

However, in July 1882 they were living in the former home of the late John Grimston at Neswick Hall, near Driffied,[49] and were still there as late as October 1884,[50] though they visited Bournemouth in the April of 1884 where their son, John Alexander, was born.[51] In November 1886 the captain was living in Scarborough[52] and in March 1889 the family was now living at Middlethorpe Hall near Bishopthorpe, to the south-east of York.[53] The family was staying in Bath on the night of the 1891 census[54] and only servants occupied Middlethorpe Hall; however the family was back at Middlethorpe Hall for the 1901 census and was still at Middlethorpe in 1905, but before May 1906 they had moved into Thicket Priory.[55] The captain and Louisa had six children, no two of which were born in the same place: daughters, Dorothy (born Wilton Street, Belgravia), Hilda (born 1 Jan 1887 in Scarborough) and Ella (born 23 May 1888 at Bishopthorpe); and sons, Mervyn (born 29 Mar 1883 at Neswick Hall, but died in infancy), John Alexander Dunnington-Jefferson, (born 10 Apr 1884 in Bournemouth), and Wilfrid Mervyn, (born 2 April 1892, at Middlethorpe Hall).

The younger brother of the captain, Thomas Trafford Dunnington-Jefferson, was a barrister. He attended school in Cheam, Surrey before going up to Trinity, Cambridge, gaining a BA in 1875; MA and LLM in 1878. He was admitted to the Inner Temple, 9 December 1874, and called to the bar, 26 January 1878.[56] Thomas died at the relatively young age of 29, 1 April 1882, at the Midland Hotel in London, but was taken back to his home parish and was buried at Thorganby.

---

leave to live there temporarily until more suitable accommodation was found for the captain and his new wife in Yorkshire

[49] BNA, *Driffield Times*, 29 Jul 1882

[50] BNA, *Beverley and East Riding Recorder*, 18 Oct 1884

[51] BNA, *London Evening Standard*, 15 Apr 1884

[52] BNA, *Yorkshire Gazette*, 13 Nov, 1886, p. 9, col. 4

[53] BNA, *York Herald*, 5 Mar 1889, p. 6, col. 1

[54] They were spending the 'season' in Bath, staying at a lodging house, 6 Catherine Place, between the Royal Crescent and the Assembly Rooms. TNA, Ref: RG12/1938, fol. 4, p. 2

[55] He mentioned this in his will, dated 6 May 1906

[56] ACAD, vol. 3, p. 557

He died intestate, and administration of his estate, which amounted to just over £1,357, was granted to his brother, Joseph John Dunnington-Jefferson.

When Joseph John and Emma were not at their Wilton Street town-house in Belgravia for the 'season' they would often entertain at Thicket Priory, which was usually reported in the newspapers of the day. Examples include a cover shoot in November 1885, where the guests included: Sir Henry and Lady Boynton, Mr. and Mrs. H. Bromley, Viscount Bangor, Colonel and Mrs. Henderson, Hon. P. Savile, Hon. Walter Maxwell, Misses Lettbridge, Hon. Martin Hawke, and Mr. Princep.[57] But it was not just the gentry and aristocracy that benefited from the largesse of the Dunnington-Jeffersons; in August 1887 they hosted a garden party where they entertained over 150 friends and neighbours from across the county. The party went on into the evening and the grounds were illuminated by large numbers of Chinese lanterns hung among the trees, and small coloured glass lamps were festooned across the lake, giving a fairy-like appearance. The evening culminated with a grand display of fireworks, and throughout music was provided by a band.[58]

Hunting and shooting at Thicket was strictly controlled by the priory's gamekeepers, but fishing was allowed, and the many fishing clubs in the York area were regularly permitted to fish the waters of the Derwent from within the grounds.[59]

Joseph John was, unsurprisingly, a dedicated Conservative, and a member of the York Conservative Association. Yearly excursions were arranged for members of the Association to Thicket Priory, and often attracted 150 members or more. The excursions were timed to coincide with the annual show and floral fête held by the cottagers of Thorganby, and East and West Cottingwith, while a band of the Yorkshire Hussars provided music. A cricket match was usually held between the Association and the priory, followed by a tea for all, altogether about four hours of pleasant entertainment. Many of those who attended were named in newspaper reports.[60]

The closing years of the century were marked by three events. The first was a change in the law which equalised the death duties on real and personal

---

[57] BNA, *Yorkshire Gazette*, 7 Nov 1885, p. 4

[58] BNA, *Yorkshire Post and Leeds Intelligencer*, 9 Aug 1887, p. 8

[59] BNA, *York Herald*, 21 Sep 1889, p. 13

[60] For example, see the following article, BNA, *Yorkshire Gazette*, 13 Aug 1892

property, the repercussions of which were only realised much later.[61] The second was a fire that had broken out at Thicket Priory in May 1897. The family was away at the time, probably in Wilton Street for the season, and only a few servants were at the house. The fire broke out in the housemaid's room, and the fire brigade was sent for and dispatched from York. Fortunately, by the time the engine had arrived at Thicket, the villagers had managed to extinguish the fire by means of buckets of water, but the housemaid's room was completely destroyed, including its furniture, and several windows had broken. It is not known if the housemaid kept her position![62] The second event was more melancholy, with the passing of Joseph John's mother, Anna Mervynia, 2 November 1898, at the good age of 86 years. Anna was buried at Thorganby,[63] leaving a will.

The new century began with news of some of the inhabitants of Thorganby with connections to the priory. In the August of 1900 the funeral took place of the 'Oldest Inhabitant' of Thorganby. Mr. Thomas Barton was buried at Thorganby, and was described as 'the oldest inhabitant of the parish, having reached the age of 89. Years ago he was a farmer in the parish under the late Canon Jefferson. For more than forty years he has been employed at Thicket Priory;'[64] and in April 1903 the sad news was announced that 'Mr. E. Carr, second keeper to Captain Jefferson, Thicket Priory, Cottingwith, has disappeared. The Derwent is being dragged.'[65] The passing of another 'oldest tenant farmer' was reported in December 1907, when the death was announced, at the advanced age of 85 years, of Mr. George Holdridge, at North Duffield Lodge. He was described as a 'well-known and highly-respected East Riding agriculturalist', and 'one of the oldest tenant farmers on Captain Jefferson's Thicket Priory Estate, and had resided at North Duffield Lodge for over 44 years.' He was buried at Skipworth churchyard.[66]

---

[61] It was Sir William Harcourt, the Liberal Chancellor, who promoted the Finance Act 1894. The bill was designed to break up large estates

[62] BNA, *Driffield Times*, 22 May 1897

[63] BNA, *London Evening Standard*, 7 Nov 1898

[64] BNA, *York Herald*, 22 Aug 1900

[65] BNA, *Yorkshire Evening Post*, 6 Apr 1903

[66] BNA, *Hull Daily Mail*, 13 Dec 1907

Returning to Thicket Priory and family affairs, July 1905 saw the start of Captain Jefferson's disposal of many of his outlying lands and cottages at Howden, Barmby on the Marsh, Bellasize, Eastrington and Bishopsoil.[67] The sales were by auction, and totalled over 1,767 acres. The sale also included the historic Manor House in Howden, formerly the palace of the Bishops of Durham when they were lords of the manor. The sale of the Manor House alone fetched £2,550. It is unclear what prompted this disposal, as land was the mainstay of the gentry at this time. Did the captain need money? The auctioneers were Richardson and Pearce-Brown of Selby (this was Reginald Pearce-Brown, formerly the land agent and estate manager at Thicket Priory).

Also in 1905 saw news of the death of Mervynia Jane Dunnington-Jefferson, the sister of the captain and eldest daughter of Canon Joseph. She resided with her cousin at Langridge Rectory, but was brought home to be buried at Thorganby.[68]

The next two items to be reported in the newspapers were curious and tragic. In December 1909 an advertisement appeared in the press:

CHAUFFEUR-GARDENER desires situation, experienced workshop and private service driving, careful driver, clean licence; 5 years experience inside and outside gardening; references; total abstainer; present master going abroad. – Matthews, Thicket Priory, York.

The master of Thicket Priory was Joseph John, and there is no sign of him or his wife Emma (they had no children) in the 1911 census. Was this the 'present master going abroad'? So where had they gone? To stay with Emma's family back in Ireland perhaps? The only person in Thicket Priory in the 1911 census was a sole butler, Frederick Matthews. Was this the chauffeur in the 1909 advertisement above?

Captain Mervyn was visiting his in-laws at the time of the 1911 census, but there was no sign of his wife, Louisa Dorothy. Was she abroad with her father-in-law? Certainly, things were not well with the captain, as the next piece of news was tragic and shocking.

---

[67] *Yorkshire Post and Leeds Intelligencer*, 7 and 8 Jul 1905; *Sheffield Daily Telegraph*, 7 Jul 1905
[68] *Clifton Society*, 8 June 1905

On the evening of Wednesday, 21 March 1912, the captain was staying at the Royal Station Hotel in York, where he was engaged in conversation with two prominent York citizens who reported that the captain appeared to be in his normal health, and afterwards seemed to be busily engaged in writing. Early the following morning he bought a first-class ticket and took the first 6.30am train to Hull. A fellow traveller on the train who knew the captain reported that the captain was restless and went to the window twice and eventually changed his compartment. The traveller reported that when he left the train at Nunburnholme the captain was still on the train.

What happened after that is something of a mystery. After passing Market Weighton station, but half a mile short of Kilingcotes station, the captain and the train parted company while the train was in full motion. It was not known at the time if he had jumped from the train, or fell accidentally. He may have been stunned from an injury he sustained behind his ear as a result of his fall from the train.

Following an inquest it was revealed that the driver and fireman on another train, coming in the opposite direction to the captain's original journey, reported that the captain deliberately walked on the rails directly towards the oncoming train, despite it sounding its horn twice. The driver applied his brakes, but it was too late and the train ran over the unfortunate captain. His injuries were horrific. A policeman was despatched from Market Weighton who identified the body on the line as that of Captain Dunnington-Jefferson. His cheque book was found three quarters of a mile nearer Market Weighton, and £3 10s in gold was found nearer the scene of the fatality. No writing was found on the body. The body of the captain was then removed to Market Weighton Station.

An inquest was held the following day when the jury heard from the witnesses, and returned a verdict that Captain Jefferson had 'committed suicide while in a state of unsound mind.'

The funeral of the captain was held on Monday, 26 March 1912, at Thorganby, the chief mourners being his widow, Louisa Dorothy, his second son Wilfrid Mervyn, his daughter Hilda, and his brother Joseph John. His eldest son, Lieutenant John Alexander, could not attend, being with his regiment in India, nor could his two other daughters, Dorothy and Ella, but no reason was given.

A great many of the county gentry, priory estate staff, tenant farmers, and many others also attended the funeral. Curiously, a Mr. and Mrs. Edwin Gray of York were prevented from attending.[69]

Captain Dunnington-Jefferson left a will, dated 5 May 1906, while he was living at Thicket Priory. He bequeathed to his wife, using her second forename of Dorothy, 'all the plate, plated articles, furniture, linen, glass, china, pictures, prints, photographs, objects of virtu or curiosity, musical instruments, books, and other articles of household use or ornament which I brought from Middlethorpe Hall'. He left all the rest of his personal estate, and all his real estate to his son, John Alexander. He appointed John Alexander and Wilfred Forbes Home Thomson of Nunthorpe executors of his will, and his wife to be the guardian of his infant children. The will was probated on 24 May 1912, at the Principal Probate Registry.

The following year on 5 May 1913, the land agent, Andrew Moscrop, acting on behalf of Joseph John Dunnington-Jefferson, put Thicket Priory up for rent, 'with early entry'. It was described as having '5 reception rooms, billiard-room, 30 bed and dressing rooms, outside laundry, and stabling for 12.'

Joseph John, now 67 years of age, and his wife, Emma, then led a quiet retirement, staying at their favourites haunts mainly in London and Bath. When Emma died in 1920 her address was given as 24 Bath Road, Reading, a fine old building, still standing today. She was then taken home and buried at Thorganby.[70] When Joseph John died in 1928 his address was given as 60 Cumberland Road, Reading,[71] but dying at Marloes Road, South Kensington, London W8.[72]

The captain's widow, Louisa Dorothy, gave her residence as Ashcroft, Old Nunthorpe, York in 1915, in the obituary for her son, Lieutenant Wilfrid Mervyn Dunnington-Jefferson, killed during WWI.[73] When Louisa Dorothy

---

[69] This was probably Edwin Gray, the York solicitor who became the Lord Mayor of York in 1897/8

[70] BI, Ref: PR–THORG–6, p. 85

[71] Address given for him during the probate process

[72] Address given in burial register: BI, Ref: PR–THORG–6, p. 90

[73] *Yorkshire Evening Post*, 5 May 1915, p. 3. The status of Ashcroft at this time is unclear, but it was later the Ashcroft Hotel. It is in the parish of St. Mary Bishophill Junior but near

died in 1951, in her 99th year, her address at that time was given as 40 Cottesmore Court, London, W8.[74] Louisa Dorothy was also buried at Thorganby.[75]

Bishopthorpe. Louisa Dorothy was listed as living at Ashcroft, Bishopthorpe, in *Kelly's Directory of N & E Ridings of Yorkshire, 1913, part 2,* but not there in the 1911 census
[74] Find A Will (online resource)
[75] BI, Ref: PR–THORG–6, p. 101

CHAPTER 3
Estate Management
William Burland – Reginald Pearce-Brown –
Andrew Moscrop – J. E. Smith – Colin Bell – Andrew Mason

Prior to the building of Thicket Priory in the 1840s, estate management was performed by solicitors or land agents on behalf of the estate owners and sometimes by the land owners themselves. They would collect the rents and renew or re-grant leases of the farms, cottages, tenements and land that comprised the estate. Shortly after the building of Thicket Priory in 1847 we hear for the first time of a local estate manager in connection with Thicket Priory, one William Burland. He first appears in the 1851 census returns, living in Thorganby Lodge and is described as 'Farm Bailiff'. In the 1861 and 1871 censuses he is still living in Thorganby and is now described as an 'Accountant'; but now a James Petty also appears, described as 'Working Bailiff'. Their actual roles and responsibilities cannot be gleaned from census returns alone, but fortunately the letter-books of the Rev. Joseph Dunnington-Jefferson and his 'agent', William Burland, survive, and make for interesting reading.[76]

The letter-books contain letters emanating from the estate office and are all from either the Reverend Joseph Dunnington-Jefferson or his estate manager, William Burland, but the letters from the Reverend are written in a variety of hands, suggesting that the Reverend wrote his letters, but before they were sent someone in the estate office copied the letters into the letter-books to keep a note of what had been written.

The letters are mixed, primarily concerning the estate, such as the purchasing of various goods and services, the hiring of staff, the collection of rents from tenants, etc., but they also contain the private letters of the Reverend Joseph, which provided some detail for the previous chapter.

The estate letters reveal that when it came to an application to acquire a farm tenancy, or an application for a household servant position, the Reverend Joseph always required references, which were all followed up by letters to the referees.

---

[76] HHC, Refs: U DDJ/40/4–10, covering the period 1855–1870

When it came to the tenancy of farms, these came directly to the estate office. Noticeably, the Reverend Joseph placed a high regard on the moral character of the applicant:

29 Feb 1864
The Rev. A Clarke, of Elvington, York.
Concerning Mr. W Brown of Elvington who has applied to me for a farm at West Cottingwith of 120 acres. Request for opinion of him. Is he a moral man, has sufficient capital for such an undertaking, viz £500 or £600. Does he and his wife have your favourable opinion, are they church people? JDJ

All applications for household servant positions came via the Register Office for Servants, Coney Street, York. A typical follow-up letter to a referee would read:

21 Apr 1865
The Rev. J. E. Sampson.
Sir, John Grainger has offered himself to me as Footman. Opinion on him please, not his professional capabilities, but his moral character JDJ

Occasionally the Reverend Joseph would be approached by a farm worker employed by one of his tenant farmers, hoping the Reverend could intervene in a grievance, which he sometimes did, as the next letter shows:

3 Apr 1865
Mr. Henry Jackson, Escrick.
Sir, George Parker of Wheldrake has complained to me that you have refused to pay him wages for 3½ days amounting to 4s. 8d. Please settle with him. JDJ

Incoming letters do not survive, only the outgoing letters in the letter-books, but sometimes the letter-books reveal the outcome of an application, as the next letter shows:

27 Apr 1865
Mr Sysworth, Register Office for Servants, Coney Street, York.
I am sorry to say that the character I have received for John Grainger is not so satisfactory as I could have wished. I will venture, however, to engage him. His wages will be twenty two pounds a year. He may be at the White House, Coppergate, on Saturday at 3 o'clock. JDJ

The letter-books occasionally contain Amalgamated Assessed Tax Returns, which contain the names of the household servants, the number of carriages and horses, the use of armorial bearings, the number of dogs, and the amount of tax or duty paid, such as this return in 1865:

Names of Servants 20/- Each	Capacity in which each Serves
Thomas Strickland	Butler
Richard Fowler	Footman
John Smillie	Coachman
George Keath	Groom
William Armitage	Groom
William Henry Roper	Gardener
James Crier	Gamekeeper
George Lancaster (duty 10/6)	Under Gamekeeper
Carriages with four wheels, duty £3 10s. 0d.	3
Carriages less than four wheels 15s. 0d.	2
Horses exceeding 13 hands £1 1s. 0d. each	8
Horses exceeding 13 hands £0 10s. 6d. each	1
Ponies, £0 5s. 3d. each	0
Armorial Bearings, used by those chargeable the duty of £3 10s. 0d. for a four-wheeled carriage - Yes	
Dogs	Six

The letter-books end in 1870, and the estate manager, William Burland, Esq., died 30 April 1876 and was buried 5 May at Brotherton. No further letter-books survive, but they were almost certainly kept.

From 1878 the Thicket Priory Estate was managed by Reginald Pearce-Brown, who lived at Thorganby Hall with his wife Edith, three sons and four servants. Reginald was an Oxford BA. He was responsible for forming the stud at Thicket of Hackneys and Shires in 1882/3, and also managed the Home Farm of over 1,000 acres. Reginald attended a great many of the agricultural shows, gaining prizes for the horses of Thicket. The 1881 census records Reginald as living at Thorganby Hall, where he is described as 'Land Agent', while James Petty, 'Farm Bailiff', is recorded at Thicket Farm House and Buildings. Reginald would often visit the stock sales in the area, particularly the stock sales of Messrs. Richardson at Selby, where Reginald would be described as 'agent to Mr. J. J. Dunnington-Jefferson, JP, Thorganby Hall.'[77]

By 1889 the stud at Thicket was one of great renown. A typical report of the stud prior to a horse sale was recorded in one of the York newspapers for March of that year:

> Mr. Jefferson has made plain his desire to improve the breed and usefulness of the horses in the possession of his own tenants and the farmers of the district. He has paid high prices for the best mares and stallions that could be obtained, and has, through his able and shrewd agent, Mr. R. Pearce-Brown, whose judgment has by results been proved to be almost faultless, secured animals which have produced progeny showing all the best characteristics of pure shire blood.[78]

The 1891 census recorded Reginald Pearce-Brown, land agent, once more residing at Thorganby Hall, but now there was a new farm bailiff, a John Bowson, residing at Thicket Farm.

In October 1892 it was time for pastures new and Reginald advertised in *The Field* magazine for another position in the country as an estate agent. The advertisement was apparently successful, as the following month a testimonial, accompanied by a cheque, was presented at Thorganby Hall, attended by a large circle of friends and tenants, but among the guest list Joseph John was noticeable by his absence.

Reginald had formed a partnership in 1893 with the proprietor of one of the livestock auctioneers, formerly known as Messrs. Richardson, of Selby,

---

[77] BNA, *Goole Times*, 8 Mar 1889, p. 8, col. 1
[78] BNA, *York Herald*, 30 Mar 1889, p. 3, col. 6

but with the passing of Mr. Richardson (the father), Mr. Richardson (the son) was also keen to form a new joint partnership. The new concern was now known as Richardson and Pearce-Brown, Auctioneers of Selby, and continued to sell and auction livestock from Thicket.

Pearce-Brown was immediatey replaced by Andrew Moscrop at Thorganby Hall, and sales of horses from the Thicket Stud were now handled by Andrew.[79] The following year Andrew married Annie Chapman, daughter of the late Eccles Haigh of Liverpool.[80]

The 1901 census records Andrew Moscrop of Thorganby Hall, land agent and auctioneer, and Edmund Gabbitas is now at Thicket Priory New Farm, as farm bailiff. As well as managing the Thicket Stud, Andrew was also responsible for acquiring additions to the estate. In August 1903, Moscrop attended an auction in Selby and purchased a parcel of land in East Cottingwith of just over 3 acres, on behalf of the Thicket Priory Estate, for £250;[81] and in March 1905 he attended an auction in York where a small farm in East Cottingwith was one of the lots. The bidding started at £2,000 and was eventually knocked down to Mr. Moscrop for £3,580.[82]

One of the unusual properties Mr. Moscrop was required to handle was Thicket Priory itself, when it was offered, furnished, with 3,500 acres of good mixed shooting, in April 1909. A pre-notice of availability 'next spring' had been advertised the previous December, possibly to coincide with the forthcoming 'season'.[83] It does not appear that there were any takers.

All tenders for repairs and alterations to estate properties, including all outlying farms etc., needed to be submitted to Mr. Moscrop for his action. The estate office at Thorganby Hall would also provide plans, drawings and specifications for viewing by prospective tenderers.[84] Occasionally, Mr.

---

[79] BNA, *Yorkshire Gazette*, 27 May 1893, p. 8, col. 1

[80] BNA, *Manchester Courier and Lancashire General Advertiser*, 20 Feb 1894, p. 8, col. 8

[81] BNA, *Leeds Mercury*, 13 Aug 1903,p. 7, col. 6

[82] BNA, *Sheffield Daily Telegraph*, 3 Mar 1905, p. 11, col. 5

[83] A pre-notice of availability, 'next spring' was advertised first, BNA, *Yorkshire Post and Leeds Intelligencer*, 5 Dec 1908, p. 4, col. 4, and the actual availability was posted in: BNA, *Yorkshire Post and Leeds Intelligencer*, 17 Apr 1909, p. 5, col. 3

[84] For example, tenders were invited for alterations and additions to a farmstead at Bullen's Hill, North Newbald, to be sent to Andrew Moscrop at Thorganby Hall, where plans and

Moscrop acted as a judge at local agricultural shows,[85] and he was an active member on the Yorkshire Agricultural Society Council.

Following the failure to find a tenant for Thicket Priory, a different tack was tried in April 1916. Instead of the priory building being offered for rent, the grounds were offered instead, where shooting in over 3,500 acres, including 125 acres of coverts, were put up for rent.[86]

Following World War I, Andrew Moscrop was awarded the OBE in the King's Birthday Honours, in June 1918, for services in connection with the war. He was described as 'a well known agriculturalist, a member of the Central Agricultural Wages Board, president of the York Board of Agriculture Advisory Committee on Food Production, a member of the Council of the Yorkshire Agricultural Society, secretary of the York Shorthorn Society, and a member of the Council of the Yorkshire Coach Horse Society, and a prominent figure in the agricultural world in the North.'

As well as these prestigious offices that Andrew Moscrop filled at Thorganby Hall, he was also responsible for the more mundane appointments of farm workers on the Thicket Priory Estate. In April 1920, for example, he advertised for a driver for a Fordson tractor, with a good cottage and garden as part of the remuneration,[87] and in January 1925 he advertised for 'a strong Youth as an Assistant' on a pedigree pig farm.[88]

Active to the end, Andrew Moscrop retired in 1933 and died 1 January 1936, aged 72, after a short illness. A widower by this time, and with no children, his passing was greatly mourned by all that knew him, and his death was recorded in all the Yorkshire newspapers of the day.[89] He was buried at Thorganby, 3 January 1936, and the service was conducted by Canon Harrison, the Chancellor of York Minster.

---

specifications could also be seen. BNA, *Yorkshire Post and Leeds Intelligencer*, 24 June 1911, p. 1, col. 7

[85] For example, he was a judge at the Easingwold Show, in the Coaching and Agricultural sections, BNA, *Yorkshire Evening Press*, 20 Sep 1911, p. 3, col. 7

[86] BNA, *Yorkshire Post and Leeds Intelligencer*, 8 Apr 1916, p. 4, col. 3

[87] BNA, *Yorkshire Post and Leeds Intelligencer*, 3 Apr 1920, p. 7, col. 3

[88] BNA, *Yorkshire Post and Leeds Intelligencer*, 22 Jan 1925, p. 2, col. 5

[89] For example, BNA, *Yorkshire Evening Post*, 1 Jan 1936, p. 9, col. 5

Andrew Moscrop left an estate worth £9, 689, and his bequests included £500 to Dr. Bernardo's Homes, and £1 to each child on the register at West Cottingwith School. He also left £20 to his servant, Mary Lynn (if still serving), and £10 to all his other servants, both indoor and outdoor; £1,000 to Annie McNeil; and £500 each to Helen McNeil and Tom H. Dobson; and £250 to his cousin, Elizabeth Taylor. The residue was left to his sisters, Jane, Margaret and Edith, during their lives, and after to York County Hospital.[90]

Thorganby House

Andrew Moscrop was succeeded by James Eric Smith who ran the estate office from 1933 to 1955, but out of Thorganby House, rather than Thorganby Hall. Thorganby House, a listed building, *circa* 1845, probably by Edward Blore,[91] was occupied by the vicar of Thorganby from 1880–1926,[92] and was located near the church and almost opposite the village hall.

---

[90] BNA, *Yorkshire Post and Leeds Intelligencer*, 28 Apr 1936, p. 3, col. 6
[91] Pevsner, Neave, p. 722

Fortunately, the daughter of James Eric Smith, Eve Smith, was available for interview at the writing of this chapter, and was able to give a great deal of detail concerning the management of the estate by her father, the land agent.

Q. How many direct employees did the estate office have?
A. The majority of the residents of Thorganby at that time were employed by the estate office, and included the bailiffs, gamekeepers, joiner, blacksmith and several others. In addition there were tractor drivers and ploughmen and other agricultural workers who worked the two farms directly under the estate, Thicket Home Farm and Thorganby Home Farm. There were only a handful of incomers to the village.
Q. Where did your father come from?
A. My father came from Northumberland and prior to Thicket he worked on the Middleton Hall Estate. Although not a qualified veterinary he took a keen interest in animal welfare and was able to administer animal first aid when the need arose.
Q. Did your father work alone in the estate office?
A. On taking up his position at the Thicket Priory Estate office my father took on a secretary, Frances Hyndsley, who proved invaluable.[93]
Q. Where was the estate office located?

---

[92] VCH, *East*, vol. 3, p. 116

[93] Advertisements for tenants for Thorganby Grange Farm, North Duffield Lodge Farm and Thorganby Hall Farm in August 1936, July 1937 and August 1938, respectively, were all placed by Mr. Smith's office, Ref: BNA, *Yorkshire Post and Leeds Intelligencer*, 1 Aug 1936; *Yorkshire Post and Leeds Intelligencer*, 17 Jul 1937; *Yorkshire Post and Leeds Intelligencer*, 20 Aug 1938. Similarly, advertisements for estate workers were placed by Mr. Smith in November 1942 (joiner), January 1944 (tractor driver), December 1944 (stockman-shepherd), July 1946 (stockman, cattle and sheep) and November 1947 (stockman, cattle and sheep), Ref: BNA, *Yorkshire Post and Leeds Intelligencer*, 28 Nov 1942, p. 6, col. 7; *Yorkshire Post and Leeds Intelligencer*, 8 Jan 1944, p. 7, col. 2; *Yorkshire Post and Leeds Intelligencer*,   December 1944, p. 4, col. 8; *Yorkshire Post and Leeds Intelligencer*, 5 Jul 1946, p. 4, col. 8; *Yorkshire Post and Leeds Intelligencer*, 24 Nov 1947, p. 3, col. 7

A. It was inside Thorganby House in a room on the right of the entrance hall.

Q. Did Thorganby House have any servants?

A. We had one full-time maid, a Frances Hardcastle, plus two ladies who came from the village daily to do cleaning work, plus a Lizzy Knot who came to do the laundry and ironing. Outside, there was a groom who looked after father's horse and the Shetland ponies which myself and my brother rode. The house had no cook, as mother liked to do her own cooking. Mother was a teacher by profession, and while at Thorganby House she started the local Women's Institute.

Q. Tell me about the house.

A. The house was large, with cellars used for storing apples, but I think it was a wine cellar previously. The cellar would often flood, up to a depth of two to three feet. On the ground floor was the estate office, drawing room, dining room, kitchen and scullery. The upper floor had around twelve rooms, ten of which served as bedrooms, and at times we shared the house with the local vicar and his family. During WWII we also hosted two young evacuees from Hull, Dick and Harry.

Q. What technical facilities did the estate office have?

A. It had a telephone.[94] There was no grid electricity to the house in 1953, but electrical power was supplied by an outside generator located in an outbuilding.

Thank you very much, Eve.

Mr. Smith continued to advertise for workers in the early 1950s. Even for general farm hands the estate office would often specify that the man should apply with references and be married. In return the estate offered a good three-bedroomed cottage in the village as part of the terms of employment.[95]

---

[94] At least by 27 April 1945, as at that date Mr. Smith advertised in the local newspapers for the return of a lost polled heifer, and asked to be informed at the estate office on Telephone: Wheldrake 13, BNA, *Yorkshire Post and Leeds Intelligencer*, 27 Apr 1945, p. 4, col. 3

[95] BNA, *Yorkshire Post and Leeds Intelligencer*, 18 Jan 1950, p. 4, col. 7

Mr. Smith, like his predecessors, also combined estate work with agricultural offices in the county and was a member of local committees. He was the Yorkshire branch secretary of the County Landowners Association from at least May 1950,[96] and chairman of the Thorganby Church Restoration Committee.[97] He also acted as land agent for other Yorkshire estates.

The last advertisement available from the British Newspaper Archive concerning the Thicket Priory Estate appeared on 29 October 1955, when Mr. Smith advertised for a 'general farm worker' offering a good house with mains water, near a school, and for '2 young single men' to live in, as second tractor driver and general farm worker.[98]

The estate office under Mr. Smith continued until 1964, when the family moved on following the sale of the Thicket Priory Estate by Sir John Dunnington-Jefferson, Bt. to Mr. John Bealby Eastwood in that year, though Mr. Smith continued to advise Mr. Eastwood's new estate manager, Colin Bell, right up to his (Mr. Smith's) death in 1976.

John Bealby Eastwood, later to become Sir John Bealby Eastwood in July 1975, and CBE in 1980[99], was born 9 January 1909 and attended the Queen Elizabeth Grammar School in Mansfield. He made his fortune in the integrated chicken and egg market and became one of the largest producers in the world. He sold the Thicket Priory Estate for around £4 million in 1978[100] and died in Farnsfield, Nottinghamshire, 6 August 1995.[101]

The Thicket Priory Estate was purchased from Sir John Bealby by Humberts, the property agents, on behalf of the British Gas Corporation Pension Fund, and they installed their own estate manager, Andrew Mason, who resided at Thorganby Hall. Over the subsequent years the houses were sold to the tenants by British Gas and the estate is now all but extinguished.[102]

---

[96] BNA, *Yorkshire Post and Leeds Intelligencer*, 8 May 1950, p. 2, col. 1

[97] BNA, *Yorkshire Evening Post*, 19 Apr 1952, p. 6, col. 1

[98] BNA, *Yorkshire Post and Leeds Intelligencer*, 29 Oct 1955, p. 11, col. 8

[99] *The London Gazette*, no. 48456, p. 17524, 18 December 1980

[100] The sale was advertised in the *Financial Times*, 5 July 1978

[101] The above brief biography was provided in his obituary, printed in *The Independent* newspaper, 4 October 1995

[102] The information in this last paragraph was kindly provided by Arturas Janusas, a resident of Thorganby and local historian

CHAPTER 4
WWI and the Priory
John Alexander Dunnington-Jefferson –
Wilfrid Mervyn Dunnington-Jefferson – Ella Dunnington-Jefferson –
Church Memorial

John (Jack to his friends) Alexander Dunnington-Jefferson, the elder son of Captain Mervyn Dunnington-Jefferson and his wife, Louisa Dorothy, was educated at Eton and attended Sandhurst, joining the 3rd Battalion Royal Fusiliers (City of London Regiment) in 1904 becoming a 2nd Lieutenant 2 March 1904 and Lieutenant 9 December 1905.[103]

He served initially in the Bermuda Garrison during the early part of 1905 but departed Bermuda for Cape Town, South Africa, aboard the HMT (Her/His Majesty's Transport, in other words a troopship) *Soudan* on 18 December 1905. Serving in South Africa for several years the battalion moved to Mauritius, which is where he was enumerated in the 1911 census, but later that year he and the 3rd moved again, this time to Lucknow in India, which prevented him from attending his father's funeral in March 1912.

Jack was promoted to captain 4 September 1912 and joined the newly formed Intelligence Corps section of the Headquarters Staff, 17 February 1915, as a temporary Major, and was graded for purposes of pay as a General Staff Officer, 2nd Grade.[104] On 12 August 1914 the embryo Corps embarked on the Olympia at Southampton for France with the British Expedition Force. Major J.A. Dunnington-Jefferson RF replaced Captain, later Field Marshal Lord Wavell as the Corps Commandant from December 1914 to February 1916 and was responsible for establishing the high reputation of the Corps during the war.[105]

During the First World War, he earned the Distinguished Service Order (DSO) in 1917 and was mentioned in despatches (MiD) six times; he also received the French Legion of Honour, the Belgian War Cross and the Italian Order of St. Maurice and St. Lazarus, among other honours. He ended the war

---

[103] Hart's annual army list, special reserve list, and territorial force list, 1913, p. 312
[104] *Supplement to the London Gazette*, 17 Feb 1915, p. 1651; *ditto*, 10 Mar 1915, p. 2464
[105] https://www.militaryintelligencemuseum.org/the-intelligence-corps

a Brevet Major and retired in 1919 as a Lieutenant Colonel.[106]

Jack's younger brother, Wilfrid Mervyn, did not fare so well. Educated at Radley College, Wilfrid went up to Christ Church in 1910 and was reading for the bar at the Inner Temple when he volunteered at the outbreak of the war in 1914. He enlisted with the rank of 2nd Lieutenant in the 7th Battalion, Royal Fusiliers and went to the front in Belgium in April 1915 attached to the 3rd Battalion, his elder brother's battalion. Wilfrid was killed in action near Gravenstafel in the Second Battle of Ypres, 25 April 1915.[107]

However, following information in a letter dated 8 May (1915) from Jack Dunnington-Jefferson to his mother and provided by Wilfrid's niece, Nicky Dunnington-Jefferson, this quote has come to light which surely verifies Wilfrid's date of death.

I went out to see the 3rd Bn. yesterday. Wilfrid was killed on the 25th April at a place called Gravenstafel, just North of Zonnebeke, near Ypres. He was buried where he fell, as it was impossible to bring away any of our officers.

2nd Lieutenant Wilfrid Mervyn Dunnington-Jefferson's address at death was given as Ashcroft, Old Nunthorpe, York.

It was not just the menfolk of the Dunnington-Jefferson family that were involved in the war effort. A sister of John Alexander and Wilfrid Mervyn, Ella Dunnington-Jefferson, was also involved.

Ella served first as a nurse and orderly at Clifford Street and Nunthorpe Hall Auxiliary Hospitals. These Voluntary Aid Detachment (VAD) hospitals were convalescent hospitals for injured and traumatised military personnel, and she must have seen much suffering. Ella then moved to T. E. Cooke's, when it opened in 1915 at Bishophill in York. This company specialised in making scientific instruments and equipment for the military, including rangefinders and surveying equipment and when they opened they took on many women to help with production.

---

[106] *Who Was Who* (online edition, Oxford University Press, December 2007)

[107] Ruvigny, p. 204. However, the probate of Wilfrid's will gives 24 Apr 1915 as the date of death, and the place of death as France or Belgium! His Medal Card at TNA gives 29 Apr 1915 for the date of death. However, the quoted letter validates the date of death given by Ruvigny

While working at Cooke's, Ella wrote a poem describing life at the instrument factory:

A MUNITION DIRGE

I was a nurse, a nurse was I,
Methought at Cooke's I'll have a try.

The rain poured down, the wind blew shrill,
O'er "Cookes-s;ss" Works on Bishophill.

I knocked upon the factory door,
I stood upon the office floor.

The manager spoke unto me:
"Munitions worker you would be"?

Quoth I, "I am a V.A.D.
But if you're kind I'll work for thee."

Quoth he — "It is a stiffish job,
You'll have to come for 17/- Bob".

"Be here quite sharp at early dawn,
And unto secrecy be sworn."

"At Bishophill you'll stay until
You faint before the awful drill."

They led me from the fated room
Into a dungeon full of gloom.

I sat upon a wooden stool,
I vowed I was an awful fool.

I painted reel, I painted drum,
I cut my hand, I pierced my thumb.

I drove the nail, I turned the screw
I did what'eer there was to do.

But when I saw the ladies there,
My heart leaped up, they were so fair.

Miss Tennant took me by the hand,
"Oh welcome to Munition Land"

"I'll give you buns, I'll give you tea,
And Chocolate Biscuits I'll give thee"

And dear Miss Carr, she said to me:
"We're only here on suffrance see"

Miss Blaylock works what'eer may hap,
She swallowed strip, she swallowed flap.

Her sister sat beside her too,
I gave here all my work to do.

Miss Turner left her home, her cats,
To work upon the old green felt mats.

Miss Dodsworth came from far-off France,
To drive the nail, discard the lance.

Her sister came from Nunthorpe, See!!
She also was a V.A.D.

And Mrs Hearder came from far,
To show what women workers are.

Miss Radcliffe sat among the paint.
And gazed on Eastern gardens quaint.

Miss Bury painted like a dear,
But on her work shed many a tear.

There was Harrison, our Overseer,
Who caused us all to quake with fear.

Oh Harri - son, Oh Harri - son,
A dreadful work you've started on.

I once did to the palace start,
With white kid gloves and quaking heart.

Where Mrs Leetham worked apace,
With Mrs Rudgard in a race.

Miss Moxon sat in queenly state,
With love of work, inborn, innate.

Miss Wright — who came from Harro-gate.
And turned up ne'er a moment late.

The Bubble-people sit below,
And bubbles all day long they blow.

Within the glass-shop, good and staid,
The skilled workers ply their trade.

And when you're feeling very low,
Oh! Come to Cooke's, Heigho!! Heigho!!

Miss Tennant dear, will give you tea,
You'll be in splendid companee.

Mid'st shower and rain in far-off Lands,
Our soldiers fight with eager hands.

We cannot join their splendid throng.
Drive back the foe, make right the wrong.

To drive the nail, to turn the screw,
Is what we women all can do.

And even, when the work is slow,
Are we at Cooke's downhearted? No!!

E. D. Jefferson

A Munition Dirge survives today in the archived records of Cooke's.[108]

The men of the parish suffered a number of losses during WWI, and the names of the men who lost their lives in what became known as the Great War have been memorialised on a plaque in St. Helen's Church.

**TO THE GLORY OF GOD AND IN MEMORY OF THE
MEN OF THIS PARISH WHO GAVE THEIR LIVES
IN THE SERVICE OF THEIR COUNTRY DURING
THE GREAT WAR 1914–1919.**

WILFRID MERVYN DUNNINGTON JEFFERSON, R. FUS., KILLED IN ACTION APRIL 25TH, 1915.
HERBERT HANLEY, COLDSTREAM GUARDS, KILLED IN ACTION SEPT. 15TH, 1916.
ARCHIE SPENCER, COLDSTREAM GUARDS, KILLED IN ACTION SEPT. 15TH, 1916.
GEORGE HENRY WILSON, ROYAL ARMY MEDICAL CORPS, KILLED IN ACTION AUGUST 19TH, 1916.
JOHN HENRY LANCASTER, WEST YORKS REGT., DIED SEPT. 12TH, 1917.
LEONARD CLAUDE GOSLEY, COLDSTREAM GDS., KILLED IN ACTION DECEMBER 5TH, 1917.
FRED DITCHBURN, ROYAL FIELD ARTILLERY, DIED JANUARY 26TH, 1918.
WILLIAM JAMES MOFFAT, ROYAL SCOTS GREYS, KILLED IN ACTION MARCH 23RD, 1918.
ARTHUR WILSON, HAMPSHIRE REGT., KILLED IN ACTION SEPTEMBER 1ST, 1918.
ARTHUR IBBOTSON THOMPSON, KING'S OWN YORKS LT. INF., DIED MAY 24TH, 1919.
NORMAN GILL COSSINS, LONDON REGT., DIED OF WOUNDS WHILE A PRISONER OF WAR.

**"MAKE THEM TO BE NUMBERED WITH THY SAINTS
IN GLORY EVERLASTING."**

---

[108] BI, Ref: Cooke, Troughton and Simms Archive

Further details on the above men are as follows:[109]

Herbert Hanley of Thorganby, Yorks, Private Coldstream Guards, Reg. No. 14506, enlisted in Newark, fought in France and Flanders, killed in action 16 September 1916.

Archie Spencer of Thorganby, Yorks, Private Coldstream Guards, Reg. No. 15542, enlisted in Pocklington, fought in France and Flanders, killed in action 15 September 1916.

George Henry Wilson of Hull, Yorks, Gunner Royal Horse Artillery and Royal Field Artillery, Reg. No. 75618, enlisted in Hull, fought in France and Flanders, killed in action 1 November 1914.

Leonard Claude Gosley, born Goodmanham, resided at Market Weighton, Yorks, Private Coldstream Guards, Reg. No. 15896, enlisted in Hull, transferred as a Guardsman to the 4th Battalion, Guards Machine Gun Regiment, Reg. No. 529, fought in France and Flanders, killed in action 16 September 1916.

Fred Ditchburn of York, Bombadier Royal Horse Artillery and Royal Field Artillery, Reg. No. 45039, enlisted in York, fought in Salonika, killed in action 26 January 1918.

William James Moffat of Hawick, Roxburgh, Corporal Household Cavalry and Cavalry of the Line (incl. Yeomanry and Imperial Camel Corps), 2nd Dragoons Battalion, (Scots Greys), fought in France and Flanders, killed in action 23 March 1918.

Arthur Wilson born West Cottingwith, residing at Howdendyke, Yorks, Private Hampshire Regiment, 10th Battalion, Reg. No. 16750, enlisted in Hull, fought in Balkans, killed in action 1 September 1918.

Arthur Ibbotson Thompson. Also commemorated on a memorial in Rawmarsh, and on a headstone in Thorganby churchyard. Husband of Emily Mary Thompson, of 13, Aldwarke Rd., Parkgate, Rotherham. Private King's Own Yorkshire Light Infantry. His service record lists that he served[110] in Germany from 18 November 1916 to 26 December 1917 and in Switzerland from 27 December 1917 until 13 June 1918. Captured near Cambrai on

---

[109] The following details have been taken from *British Soldiers Died in the Great War, 1914–1919,* www.Myheritage.com (£charge)

[110] 'Served' here was a euphemism for prisoner of war

18 November 1916. Recorded as POW at Limburg, Hesse on 17 April 1917, at Worms, Hesse on 23 July 1917 and Weiler (?) on 25 February 1918. On his return home in June 1918 he was assessed for future service and was discharged as unfit in July 1918, suffering from TB contracted during his period as a POW.[111]

Norman Gill Cossins, born Topcliffe, residing at Thorganby, Yorks, Private Royal Fusiliers (City of London Regiment) 3rd Battalion, Reg. No. 67621, enlisted in Selby, fought in France and Flanders, killed in action 26 October 1917.

It is to be regretted that no roll of honour to those who served in WWI and survived, has been attempted.

---

[111] Details from the Imperial War Museum's *Lives of the First World War* website © IWM: https://livesofthefirstworldwar.iwm.org.uk/lifestory/4415922

CHAPTER 5

The Inter-War Years

John Alexander Dunnington-Jefferson – Problems finding Tenants –
Changes at Thicket – A Marriage – Trouble in Europe

Following the end of WWI and his retirement from his regiment, Lieutenant Colonel John Alexander Dunnington-Jefferson returned to his home in Thicket Priory to pursue a public service career in local county affairs.[112] First on his agenda, however, was to get the Thicket Priory Estate back into shape. During the war years there had been a dearth of available workers both inside and outside of the priory despite many advertisements,[113] and the situation immediately after the war had not improved.[114] Perhaps a shortage of tenant farmers also led to the colonel putting five freehold farms belonging to the estate up for sale in September 1919. Only one was sold, Northfield House Farm with 148 acres of land, the incumbent tenant, Thomas Watson, jun. selling for £3,000.[115]

Less than two years later the colonel and his uncle, Joseph John, decided to disentail Thicket Priory and convert it to a fee simple, which was usually done if the intent was to eventually sell the property.[116]

---

[112] Although some newspapers reported that John Alexander Dunnington-Jefferson's career was in politics, this is not strictly true. His career reflected his main interests: county matters, agriculture, education and finance and his lifetime after the First World War was devoted to public service in these fields

[113] E.g. BNA, *Yorkshire Post and Leeds Intelligencer*, 10 May 1916; *Yorkshire Post and Leeds Intelligencer*, 10 Nov 1916; *Yorkshire Post and Leeds Intelligencer*, 2 Dec 1916; *Yorkshire Evening Post*, 8 Dec 1916; *Yorkshire Evening Post*, 4 Apr 1917; *Yorkshire Post and Leeds Intelligencer*, 11 Jul 1917

[114] General servants were in very short supply, as were housekeepers, gardeners, etc. E.g. BNA, *Yorkshire Evening Post*, 1 Mar 1919; *Yorkshire Evening Post*, 10 May 1919; *Yorkshire Post and Leeds Intelligencer*, 26 Aug 1919; *Yorkshire Post and Leeds Intelligencer*, 13 Sep 1919

[115] BNA, *Leeds Mercury*, 18 Sep, 1919

[116] Land Registry: the disentailing deed was dated 28 February 1921, and involved John Alexander Dunnington-Jefferson, of the one part; Joseph John Dunnington-Jefferson, of the

Some semblance of normality did start to appear in the 1920s. The Thicket Priory football team, The Priors, were back in action, playing away at Barmby Moor, but they were two men short due to harvesting and substitutes had to be found.[117] Unfortunately, there was some sad news in March 1928, when the colonel's uncle, Joseph John Dunnington-Jefferson, died. At the time of his death his residence was given as 28 Marloes Road, South Kensington, London W.8. Joseph John was brought home to Thicket and was buried at Thorganby, 26 March 1928, aged 82.[118]

On the public service front, the colonel became a member of the Yorkshire Agricultural Society in 1921 and vice chairman of the society in 1923. In 1934 he accepted the office of Honorary Show Director of the Great Yorkshire Show. In 1951 the society was the first in England to acquire a permanent showground thanks to the colonel—at Harrogate. He then served as Honorary Show Director 1934 to 1963, becoming president of the society in 1953 and 1966. He was particularly proud of his Berkshire pigs which won many awards at the Yorkshire Show and the Royal Show.

The colonel also made some changes at Thicket Priory itself. He leased the priory for a five-year term to another colonel and his family, Lieutenant Colonel C. G. Maude and his wife in 1928, and they had a son born in 1926 while living at the priory.[119] In 1930 another family occurs, giving their address as Thicket Priory, when Mr. John Wingfield Ford, the only son of Mr. and Mrs. Edward Vyvyan Ford, of Thicket Priory, was married to Miss Vera Hall Chalker, only daughter of Mr. and Mrs. Henry Chalker of Medindie, Sandal.[120]

The early 1930s were marked by two unfortunate events. In August 1930 the York Fire Brigade had to be called out again, but this time at Home Farm, Thicket Priory, when the brigade had to work for 10 hours to put out a fire at a Dutch barn of eight sections full of the season's hay; and in September 1831

---

second part; and Wilfrid Forbes Home Thomson, of the third part. A subsequent Vesting Deed releasing all rights from the right heir (John Alexander), and the trustee (Wilfrid F. H. Thomson), back to Joseph John, was entered into 1 March 1926

[117] BNA, *Hull Daily Mail*, 10 Oct 1922

[118] BI, Ref: PR–THORG–6, p. 90

[119] BNA, *Yorkshire Evening Post*, editions of 12 Oct 1926 and 20 Jun 1951

[120] BNA, *Yorkshire Post and Leeds Intelligencer*, 25 Jun 1930

a verdict of 'accidently drowned' was returned at an inquest into the death of little John Hearn, the son of the head gardener at Thicket, who drowned in the Derwent while fishing with his playmates.[121]

On the estate side of things Thicket was still having problems finding tenants for its farms. Lawns House Farm at North Duffield was advertised in September 1930, then again in February 1932 and September 1932, while an advertisement in August 1932 offered 'Some Farms of handy sizes' to be let from Lady Day 1933,[122] and another offered Woodfield Farm of 45 acres of grass and 199 acres of arable, also in the advertisement of September 1932.

Lawns House Farm was offered yet again in January 1934 along with Thorganby Hall Farm, which itself was offered again in September 1934.[123] Clearly, finding and retaining tenant farmers was certainly an onerous task for the estate manager, Andrew Moscrop, in the inter-war years.

The mid-1930s saw two more deaths. In November 1935 Mr. Arthur Thomas Farr, aged 69, a joiner on the estate, was found dead in the estate workshop, having been employed on the estate for 53 years;[124] and in January 1936 Andrew Moscrop, Esq., the estate manager and land agent also died. He was a widower with no children, and his passing was a great loss to the estate and to the many organisations of which he was a member. He was 72.[125]

Andrew Moscrop was succeeded as estate manager by James Eric Smith, but he managed the estate out of Thorganby House rather than Thorganby Hall, as has been stated earlier. Mr. Smith was always known as Jim Smith.

Some significant events in the life of Colonel Jefferson also occurred over the same period. When the lease to Colonel Maude of the priory expired in 1933 the building was unoccupied for more than five years, and was

---

[121] BNA, *Hull Daily Mail*, 4 Sep 1931

[122] BNA, *Yorkshire Post and Leeds Intelligencer*, 13 Sep 1930; *Yorkshire Post and Leeds Intelligencer*, 20 Feb 1932; *Yorkshire Post and Leeds Intelligencer*, 6 Aug 1932; *Yorkshire Post and Leeds Intelligencer*, 10 Sep 1932

[123] BNA, *Yorkshire Evening Post*, 27 Jan 1934; *Yorkshire Post and Leeds Intelligencer*, 8 Sep 1934

[124] BNA, *Sunderland Daily Echo and Shipping Gazette*, 1 Nov 1935

[125] BNA, *Yorkshire Evening Post*, 1 Jan 1936

unoccupied in The 1939 Register,[126] a sad state of affairs.[127] In May 1935 John Dunnington-Jefferson was elected Chairman of the East Riding County Council and in December 1936 he was appointed as the new Deputy Lord Lieutenant of the East Riding of Yorkshire.[128]

The biggest events, however, were still to come in 1938, and also made clear who was now living at Thorganby Hall:

Lieut.-Colonel to Wed
The engagement is announced between Lieut.-Col. J. A. Dunnington-Jefferson, D.S.O., eldest son of the late Captain M. Dunnington-Jefferson of Thicket Priory, York, and Mrs. Dunnington-Jefferson, 40 Cottesmore Court, London, W.8, and Isobel, daughter of Lieut.-Col. H. A. Cape, D.S.O. of Thorganby Hall, York.[129]

Thorganby Wedding: Colonel Dunnington-Jefferson and Miss Isobel Cape
The marriage of Lieut-Colonel J. A. Dunnington Jefferson and Miss Isobel Cape, younger daughter of Lieut.-Colonel H. A. Cape, and the late Mrs Cape, of Thorganby Hall, took place very quietly on Saturday at Thorganby.
Owing to the critical situation earlier in the week, arrangements previously made for the wedding to take place in London were cancelled. Only relatives, personal friends and tenants and employees on the Thicket Priory Estate were present.[130]

The 'critical situation' referred to was the ongoing meeting between Prime Minister Neville Chamberlain and German Chancellor Adolf Hitler in Berchtesgaden in an attempt to negotiate an end to German expansionist policies, and the warning that England and France gave to Czechoslovak President Edvard Beneš to tell him Britain and France would not fight Hitler if he decided to annex the Sudetenland by force. While at home, Winston Churchill warned of grave consequences to European security if Czechoslovakia was partitioned.

War seemingly had been averted when Chamberlain signed the Munich

---

[126] The 1939 Register was taken on 29 September 1939. The information was used to produce identity cards and, once rationing was introduced in January 1940, to issue ration books https://www.nationalarchives.gov.uk/help-with-your-research/research-guides/1939-register/

[127] BNA, *Yorkshire Evening Post*, 20 Jun 1951

[128] BNA, *Hull Daily Mail*, 30 Dec 1936

[129] BNA, *Dundee Evening Telegraph*, 30 July 1938

[130] BNA, *Leeds Mercury*, 3 October 1938

Agreement with Hitler, and returned to the UK on the 30 September waving the Agreement and giving the now infamous speech in Downing Street, declaring *Peace in our Time*.[131]

The Munich Agreement was signed by Nazi Germany, the United Kingdom, the French Third Republic, and the Kingdom of Italy. It provided 'cession to Germany of the Sudeten German territory' of Czechoslovakia. Most of Europe celebrated the Agreement, because it prevented the war threatened by Adolf Hitler by allowing Nazi Germany's annexation of the Sudetenland, a region of western Czechoslovakia inhabited by more than three million people, mainly German speakers. Hitler announced it was his last territorial claim in Europe, and the choice seemed to be between war and appeasement. It included a resolution to resolve all future disputes between the two countries through peaceful means.

It was all an illusion.

---

[131] https://en.wikipedia.org/wiki/1938_in_the_United_Kingdom

CHAPTER 6
WWII and the Priory
Farms to Let – One Death, One Birth – Vice Lieutenant – Land Army

The United Kingdom declared war on Germany on 1 September 1939 following Germany's invasion of Poland in full breach of their commitments in the Munich Agreement.

In 1939 there was only one male in the Dunnington-Jefferson family, Lieutenant Colonel John Alexander Dunnington-Jefferson, but he had retired from the army back in 1919 and was ineligible for call-up, but that did not stop him from taking on several civilian roles to support the war effort.

The colonel, who was Chairman of the East Riding County Council, was further appointed to be the Chairman of the East Riding War Agricultural Executive Committee,[132] which had its headquarters in St. Mary's Manor in Beverley and was composed of several departments: Cultivation Department, which was mainly concerned with seeing that all land was properly cultivated, with eight district officers, who went round and knew the area and made recommendations about the cultivation orders; the Milk Department, whose job was to see that as much milk was produced from the cows as possible; the Livestock Department, whose remit was to improve the quality of livestock; the Labour Department who had the supervision of POWs (mainly Italian, but some German POWs also) and the Land Army girls, finding them accommodation and directing them to various places; and the Demonstrations Department, whose function was to introduce the most modern and up-to-date farming techniques and new machinery to the farmers of the East Riding. Farmers who did not follow the directives of the committee by failing to maximise output from their land under cultivation could be, and were, ejected from their farms and replaced. One farmer, a Mr. Mason, was ejected from his farm in Birdsall for failing to manure his land properly, and his tenancy terminated.[133] The committee certainly took their goals seriously.

---

[132] The date of the appointment has not yet been found, but he was certainly in post 22 September 1939, BNA, *Yorkshire Post and Leeds Intelligencer*, 22 Sep 1939

[133] House of Commons, *Hansard*, vol. 372, 26 June 1941, items 48/49

The estate management continued as normal during the war years, attempting to find new tenants for the estate's farms, such as Thorganby Hall Farm and Ings View Farm, both in April 1940.[134]

At family level, the colonel was bereaved of his great-aunt, Theodosia Dunnington-Jefferson, who died at the grand age of 92 in London. She had not lived in the Thicket Priory area for many years following the death of her father, the Rev. Joseph Dunnington-Jefferson. Theodosia left an estate valued at £8,255 and bequeathed £50 to Peter the cat and Billy the dog. She made several other charitable bequests and some poignant bequests to the staff of the hotel where she had been living, stating "I wish to thank them for the great humane kindness that they have always shown to me and made a lonely soul happier."[135]

In 1941, on 12 February, Jack Dunnington-Jefferson was to celebrate the birth of his first child, a daughter, Rosemary Nicolette Dunnington-Jefferson, followed by the birth of his second child, a boy, Mervyn Stewart Dunnington-Jefferson, 5 August 1943.

At priory staff level, the colonel began to advertise for a chauffeur in June 1941 for his daily commute to Beverley and occasional trips to York and other places where his duties took him. The applicant needed to be over military age, or exempt from service, and a cottage would be provided. The post was advertised again in August 1941.[136]

In December 1942 the colonel was to be promoted yet again, when his role of Deputy Lieutenant of the East Riding of Yorkshire was made up to vice-lieutenant to act in the absence of the Lieutenant of the County, Colonel Michael Guy Percival Willoughby, 11th Baron Middleton, who commanded the 5th and 30th Battalions of the East Yorkshire Regiment during WWII.

Returning to the war effort, the labour shortage on farms had become extremely acute by May of 1941 so the colonel, as Chairman of the East Riding War Agricultural Executive Committee, placed advertisements in the Yorkshire newpapers advising farmers who were short of labour to employ the ladies of the Women's Land Army (WLA).[137] The take-up of the ladies of

---

[134] BNA, *Yorkshire Post and Leeds Intelligencer*, 21 Oct 1939; 13 Jan 1940; 2 March 1940
[135] BNA, *Yorkshire Evening Post*, 11 Apr 1942
[136] BNA, *Yorkshire Post and Leeds Intelligencer*, 7 Jun 1941; 13 Aug 1941
[137] BNA, *Yorkshire Post and Leeds Intelligencer*, 17 May 1941

the WLA was slow, and resisted by some farmers, so the colonel appealed again in the March of 1942, reminding farmers that there were no reserves whatever of skilled men and that alternative forms of unskilled labour must now be sought, and directed them once more to the WLA.[138]

The war effort did, however, provide new opportunities for skilled but dying trades. The village blacksmith, whose skills were becoming less and less in demand, with only the occasional horse to shoe owing to the wholesale replacement of horses by the motor car and tractor, was given a lifeline by the war. Vehicles and farm machinery of all sorts were employed in the war effort, and when, for example, a cog lost a tooth it was a costly and time-consuming exercise to get the cog replaced. Some forward thinking brains in the Ministry of Agriculture had the idea to retrain the village blacksmiths in welding techniques, not a huge jump from the traditional blacksmith skills, but it meant that cogs and other mechanical parts could now be repaired on the spot rather than waiting for replacement parts. George Simpson, Thorganby's blacksmith, was one such smith that benefited from this retraining and became an important war worker. He obtained his proficiency certificate in oxyacetylene welding and could then repair tractors and any other type of farm machinery, raising his status and demand considerably in the locality. George's son, Geoffrey, a 16-year-old lad, had already spent two years at technical college and now joined his father in tractor classes, while George found time to give lectures to other craftsmen of the benefits of retraining.[139]

It would appear that the earlier pleas to farmers in 1941 and 1942 to utilise the labour provided by the WLA had borne fruit, and there was now a large contingent of WLA girls in the county, under the direction of the East Riding Committee, the chairman of which was the colonel's wife, Frances Isobel Dunnington-Jefferson,[140] who was also made a Justice of the Peace in December, 1944.[141]

Following Victory in Europe, on 8 May 1945, it was time to honour the efforts of the East Riding agricultural workers in the war effort.

---

[138] BNA, *Yorkshire Post and Leeds Intelligencer*, 7 Mar 1942

[139] BNA, *Yorkshire Post and Leeds Intelligencer*, 1 Jan 1943

[140] BNA, *Driffield Times*, 6 Feb 1943

[141] BNA, *Hull Daily Mail*, 19 Dec 1944

Lieutenant Colonel Dunnington-Jefferson had already been rewarded with a knighthood, 8 June 1944,[142] but the girls of the WLA also received recognition, via Armlets, with Winifred Preston, c/o Mrs. Hesslewood of Thicket Priory Lodge being one such recipient.[143]

Unfortunately, there is no memorial to the fallen of WWII in Thorganby or any list of those who served. This may be due to censorship at the time.

---

[142] BNA, *The London Gazette*, Issue 36620, 21 July 1944, p. 3416
[143] BNA, *Hull Daily Mail*, 18 Jan 1946

CHAPTER 7
The Post-War Years

Sir John Alexander Dunnington-Jefferson – Thicket Priory to be Sold –
Return of the Nuns – Sir John Bealby Eastwood – Thicket Estate Sold

The problems with finding new tenants for the farms of the Thicket Priory Estate and finding domestic staff has been discussed in the previous chapters. The upheavals of the two World Wars, combined with alternative work such as factory, retail and clerical employment for women, saw a huge fall in numbers of residential servants. The end was in sight as the few domestic servants that still were available were increasingly unwilling to 'live in'. Incomes for large estates had fallen dramatically, due to these factors, and it was perhaps in response to this that the Dunnington-Jefferson family sought new ways of monetising their assets.

In April 1951 Sir John and Lady Dunnington-Jefferson opened the gardens of Thicket Priory to visitors, on Saturdays and Sundays, 2pm to 7pm, at a charge of one shilling. Perhaps a decision had already been made, as two months later the announcement was made in the press that the priory, with its fifteen acres of land and two-acre lake was for sale, Sir John and Lady Dunnington-Jefferson and their two children intending to live in Thorganby Hall.[144] However, a buyer could not be found.

In April 1953 St Helen's Church in Thorganby was in urgent need of restoration, requiring £2,300. The villagers had managed to raise (over three years) £1,500 towards the cost. In response, Sir John and Lady Dunnington-Jefferson again decided to open the gardens at Thicket Priory and also part of the house to visitors. The gardens were in full bloom with daffodils, bouquets of which were on sale together with a country produce stall; and in the house Sir John had provided access to his collection of Flemish and Dutch paintings. The open day at Thicket managed to raise £190 towards the church restoration fund.[145]

Eventually, in 1954, a buyer was found for Thicket Priory: Carmelite nuns who needed a new home from their site in Exmouth. The Prioress, Mother Mary of Saint-John Vavasour, came from Yorkshire—her family home had

---

[144] BNA, *Yorkshire Evening Post*, 20 Jun 1951
[145] BNA, *Yorkshire Post and Leeds Intelligencer*, editions of 6 Apr 1953; 16 Apr 1953

been Hazlewood Castle. She felt drawn to relocate the community to the north of England. The sale was subject to vacant possession, so in May 1954 the entire contents of Thicket Priory were put up for auction:[146]

By order of Lieut.-Colonel Sir John
Dunnington-Jefferson, D.S.O.
THICKET PRIORY, THORGANBY, YORK
HENRY SPENCER and SONS will sell by
Auction in A MARQUEE ON THE PREMISES
on THURSDAY and FRIDAY, MAY 27 and 28.
A LARGE PORTION OF THE
CONTENTS of the HALL
including EXCELLENT PURNITURE.
A cut glass Chandelier with 12 scrolled branches for electric candles, English, Continental and Oriental decorative Porcelain, including a Crown Derby Dinner Service (138 pieces), fine Dessert Services, a Worcester Barr, Flight and Barr Tea Service, items of Davenport, Leeds, Sevres, Minton, Capo-di-Monte, Staffordshire, Delft and Chinese Porcelain, Silver and Plate, Carpeting and Rugs, Venetian and English Table Glass, Curtains, Linen, the Library of Books, Oil Paintings by or attributed to Melchior, Hondecooter, Peter Wouvermans, John Wycke, John Molenaer, L. Hubner, Sir Godfrey Kneller, Pictures of the Dutch and Italian Schools, Naval Prints, Colour Prints and Engravings, an Armstrong-Siddeley Atlanta Saloon Car, 1937 model, Kitchen and Outside Effects and Miscellanea.
Sale to commence at 11.30 a.m. promptly each day
VIEW DAY SATURDAY, MAY 22,
from 10.30 a.m until 5 p.m. by illustrated catalogue only (2s. each) which admits two persons.
Also ON VIEW on the MORNING OF SALE.
Light refreshments at reasonable charges.
HENRY SPENCER and SONS, Auctioneers.

Following the removal of the contents of Thicket Priory, the Carmelites began moving into their new home during the latter half of 1955, the conveyance being completed on 12 December of that year.[147] The story of the

---

[146] BNA, *Yorkshire Post and Leeds Intelligencer*, 15 May 1954
[147] East Riding Registry of Deeds, Beverley, vol. 102, p. 251, no. 208

move to Thicket is told in the book *Countryside & Cloister: Reminiscences of a Carmelite Nun* by Marie T. Litchfield.

After almost eight centuries, nuns were once again resident in Thicket Priory, just yards away from the site of the original priory.

Following the sale of Thicket Priory, Sir John and his family moved into Thorganby Hall, and Mr. Smith, the estate manager, continued to manage the estate farms and lands until the 1960s.

Sir John sold the remainder of the estate in 1964, comprising 3,080 acres in Thorganby and West Cottingwith, to John Bealby Eastwood, thus ending the long and distinguished tenure of the Dunnington-Jefferson family.[148]

---

[148] VCH, *East*, pp. 112–120, fn. 62

CHAPTER 8
Subsequent Ownership and Thicket Priory IV
*The Nuns at Thicket Priory III – Thicket Priory IV Built –
Thicket Priory III sold to the Corrie Family*

In 2005 the Carmelite nuns celebrated their 50 years at Thicket Priory III and a plaque to mark the event was commissioned and installed on a wall, the precise location of which has been lost to memory. However, it became clear to the nuns that the maintenance of such a large house was untenable and simply too big for their needs. In January 2006 they decided to move to a smaller and more practical monastery, better suited to their requirements. Thicket Priory III and a part of the surrounding land was sold as a private residence, and the nuns then commissioned the building of a new monastery on the land they had retained, within the walls of what had been the Victorian kitchen garden—used as such when Sir John and his family lived at the priory— closer to the site of the original Thicket Priory. This included the burial ground of the original Cistercian nuns.

The planning application for this new monastery, which I will now refer to as Thicket Priory IV, gained widespread support from the local surrounding villages who wished the nuns to stay as 'a praying presence'. Planning permission was granted in December 2007 and the sale of Thicket Priory III could then be completed. The new owner Bruce Corrie agreed not to take physical possession, in order that the nuns could continue living at Thicket Priory until they built there new monastery and could take up residence.

Building work on the new monastery then began in early 2008 with the construction of a new driveway to the site, and the cordoning off of the original Cistercian burial ground. The construction of the main building commenced in June 2008. The site manager was Dave Taylor, and together with Mary of Carmel they attended all the site meetings between the architects and contractors, having been involved throughout the planning and building process. All the nuns walked to the site each Sunday to view the progress and would often have a meal close to the kitchen garden. During the digging of the foundations an old well was discovered, and this was restored and preserved.

The new building was designed for a community of fifteen and research showed that the original Cistercian foundation had space for fifteen choir nuns. In January 2009 a service was held for the blessing and rededication of the 'new' bell before being set in place above the new chapel. The bell actually dated from 1640 and was kindly donated by the neighbouring Anglican parish of Saint Helen, Wheldrake, and several parishioners attended the rededication service, with the bell being renamed 'Joseph'.

The work on the monastery slowed during the frosty winter months, but restarted in earnest in the spring. Four stained glass windows had been designed by a local glazier, Joseph Burton, for the chapel at Thicket Priory III in 1997, and these were removed and installed in the new chapel. In the Easter of 2009 a large congregation attended the Vigil in the new chapel, including many of the Anglican friends and people who had worked on the building. The landscaping and internal fittings of the new monastery were then completed and the official handover from the construction company, Hobson and Porter of Hull, to the Carmelites took place 18 May 2009. The nuns were then able to move into their new purpose-built monastery which took place three days later.

A less academic and more narrative version of the three combined booklets in this series is currently in production. It is a large, glossy, hardback book and will include a number of photographs, maps and plans, scans of historical documents, coats of arms and illustrations to give a fuller appreciation of the priory. It will be entitled, *Thicket Priory: A History*.

Colin B. Withers

Family Wills
Note: The years given are when probate was granted, not when the will was written

Name	Date	Type
John Dunnington-Jefferson	1840	Will
Jane Dunnington	1863	Will
Rev. Joseph Dunnington-Jefferson	1880	Will
Thomas Trafford Dunnington-Jefferson	1882	Admon
Anna Mervynia Dunnington-Jefferson	1898	Will

Will of John Dunnington-Jefferson, 1840

BI, Ref: Prob. Reg. 202, fol. 403, dated 2 Aug 1834, probate 16 Dec 1840

This is the last Will and Testament of me John Dunnington Jefferson of Thorganby Hall in the County of York Esquire which I make and Publish as follows (that is to say).

In the first place I order and direct that all my just debts funeral expenses and other charges of the probate of this my will and also the several legacies or sums of money hereinafter given and bequeathed by me shall be paid discharged and taken out of my personal estate by my Executer hereinafter named with all convenient speed after my decease.

And in the next I give and bequeath all my Household goods and furniture plate linen china Books Pictures Prints Wines Spirits and other things of a household or personal nature in upon or belonging to my Mansion House called Thorganby Hall situate at Thorganby aforesaid (save and except such fixtures as are attached to the Freehold thereof) unto my brother Thomas Dunnington of Ardwick in the parish of Manchester in the County of Lancaster Esquire and my sister Jane Dunnington of Thorganby aforesaid Spinster in case both of them shall be living at the time of my decease to and for his and her own use and benefit absolutely for ever the same to be equally divided between them as tenants in common share and share alike. But in case either of them my said Brother and Sister shall happen to die during my lifetime Then I give and bequeath the whole of the said Household goods and furniture matters and things aforesaid unto the survivor of them to and for his or her sole use and benefit.

And if both of them my said Brother and Sister shall happen to be dead at the time of my decease Then and in such case I give and bequeath the whole of such household goods and furniture and all other the matters and things comprised in the aforesaid bequest to my nephew The Reverend Joseph Dunnington the younger (the eldest son of my brother Joseph Dunnington) his executors, administrators and assigns absolutely for ever.

I give and devise unto my said Brother Thomas Dunnington and Sister Jane Dunnington all that my said capital Messuage or Mansion House called Thorganby Hall situate at Thorganby aforesaid in which I now reside with the fixtures therein and the Barns Stables and other outbuildings Gardens Orchards shrubberies rights members and appurtenances belonging thereto or used therewith To hold the same to them my said Brother and Sister and their assigns for and during the term of their joint natural lives and the life of the survivor of them (without impeachment of waste) they he or she keeping the same premises in good repair and condition And in case my said sister shall happen to survive my said Brother Thomas and shall continue to reside at Thorganby Hall aforesaid then and in such case it is my wish and intention that she my said sister shall hold and enjoy therewith during such time as she shall so reside there but no longer such quantity of land belonging to me situate at Thorganby aforesaid as she chooses to occupy not exceeding thirty statute acres exclusive of Garden Ground Shrubberies and Plantations without paying any rent or other consideration for the same and I hereby give devise and bequeath to her the use and enjoyment thereof accordingly.

I give and devise all that my Manor or reputed Manor of Thorganby in the said County of York with its quit and other rents rights royalties members privileges and appurtenances and also all my Messuages Cottages Closes lands tenements rents hereditaments and real Estates situate in the Township of Thorganby aforesaid (save and except the Rectory of Thorganby) subject to the aforesaid life estate and interest of my said Sister in part of the same hereditaments And also subject as to a certain other part of my said lands and hereditaments in Thorganby hereinafter particularly described to certain annual payments to or for the Curate and the Poor of Thorganby and otherwise as hereinafter mentioned unto my said Brother Thomas Dunnington and his assigns for and during the term of his natural life (without impeachment of waste) and from and immediately after his decease give and devise the said Capital Messuage or Mansion House called Thorganby Hall with the fixtures therein and also the said Manor of Thorganby and also all my Messuages lands tenements rents and hereditaments with their respective rights members and appurtenances situate in Thorganby aforesaid (subject nevertheless and without prejudice to the life estate and interest of my said sister in such part or parts thereof as are hereinbefore mentioned And also subject as to a certain other part thereof to the said annual payments to or for the Curate and poor of Thorganby and otherwise as hereinafter mentioned) to my said nephew the Reverend Joseph Dunnington the younger to hold the same to him the said Joseph Dunnington the younger his heirs and assigns absolutely for ever.

I also give and devise unto my said nephew Joseph Dunnington the younger all that the Advowson of the Rectory of Thorganby aforesaid with the rights privileges and appurtenances thereto belonging To hold the same to him my said nephew Joseph his heirs and assigns forever I also give and devise to him my said nephew all that my Messuage Tenement or Farm house with the outbuildings and appurtenances thereto belonging situate in the Township of West Cottingwith in the said County of York and also all those several Closes fields or parcels of land thereto belonging or usually held therewith as the same Farm house Closes fields or parcels of land and hereditaments are now occupied by John Simpson as tenant thereof to or under me And also all that piece or parcel of land belonging to me containing fourteen acres one rood or thereabouts be the same more or less situate in the North Ings in the township of West Cottingwith aforesaid and now in my own occupation to hold the same hereditaments and premises to him the said Joseph Dunnington the younger his heirs and assigns absolutely forever.

I give devise and bequeath unto my nephew John Dunnington (the youngest son of my said Brother Joseph) all and singular my Messuages Cottages lands tenements rents and hereditaments and parts or shares of Messuages Cottages lands tenements rents and hereditaments whatsoever whether Freehold of inheritance or for lives Copyhold or Leasehold and whether in possession reversion remainder or expectancy situate and being in the several Townships Parishes or places of West Cottingwith (save and except the said Farm and hereditaments in the occupation of John Simpson and the said piece or parcel of land containing fourteen acres one rood or thereabouts hereinbefore devised to my said nephew Joseph) East Cottingwith, Wheldrake, Skipwith, Barlby and Hambleton in the said county of York or elsewhere (not otherwise devised or disposed of by this my will) with their and every of their rights members and appurtenances To hold the same unto him my said nephew John Dunnington his heirs and assigns absolutely for ever or for and during all my estate and interest therein according to the respective natures or qualities thereof respectively.

And Whereas I have lately entered into a contract in writing with the Trustees of [blank] Nottingham of Latham in the paid County of York farmer for the purchase of a piece or parcel of land situate in the North Ings in West Cottingwith aforesaid containing about two acres but the same has not yet been conveyed to me. Now I hereby give and devise the said piece or parcel of land and all my estate and interest therein unto and to the use of my said nephew John Dunnington his heirs and assigns for ever and in case I should happen to die before the Conveyance thereof is made and executed I direct the purchase money for the same to be paid out of my personal estate and the Conveyance to be made and executed to my said nephew.

And whereas I time ago purchased from one Benjamin Halley a moiety of an Estate situate in Thorganby aforesaid and also a moiety of the Rectory of Thorganby subject to the payment of a moiety of the yearly sum of thirty five pounds to or for the Curate of the Parish Church of Thorganby aforesaid the further yearly sum of two pounds to or for the use of the poor of the same parish And a yearly fee farm or quitrent of six pounds seven shillings and six pence or thereabouts charged upon the said estate and I have since purchased from one Richard Abby the other moiety of the Rectory of Thorganby subject to the future payment by me of the other moiety of the said last mentioned yearly sums and given to the said Richard Abby my Bond or obligation in writing for securing the due payment thereof by me and indemnifying him therefrom Now I hereby declare my will to be that the said moiety of the said Estate so purchased by me of the said Benjamin Halley shall from henceforth stand and be charged with the future payment of the whole of the said yearly sums of Thirty five pounds two pounds and six pounds seven shillings and six pence or such other or sums as may be charged on the said Estate in respect thereof And I hereby charge and make chargeable my said moiety of the said Estate with the payment of the said several sums of money accordingly.

And as to all and every the Messuages lauds tenements rents and hereditaments whatsoever which I now am or at the time of my decease shall be seized of as mortgagee for any Estate of Freehold I give and devise the same with their and every of their appurtenances and all my estate and interest therein unto and to the use of my said Brother Thomas Dunnington his heirs and assigns upon trust and to the intent that he my said brother or his heirs shall on payment to him so my Executor hereinafter named of such sum or sums of money as shall be due and owing upon or in respect of the several mortgages and securities affecting or charging the same respective premises so in mortgage to me as aforesaid which ought to be paid to my executors or administrators convey and assure the several and respective hereditaments and premises which I am or shall be so seized as mortgagee as aforesaid with their and every of their appurtenances unto and to the use of the person or persons his her or their heirs and assigns who at the time or several times of making such payment respectively shall be respectively entitled to the redemption or equity of redemption of and in the said respective mortgaged premises but the monies which shall be received for or in respect of the said several mortgages and securities I order and direct to be paid and applied for such uses intents and purposes as are mentioned and directed in and by this my will concerning my personal estate and in aid thereof and as to all and every the Messuages lands tenements rents and hereditaments whereof I now am or at the time of my decease shall be seized or entitled in trust for any person or persons whomsoever I give and devise the same with their and every of their appurtenances unto and to the use of my said Brother Thomas his heirs and assigns upon such and the same trusts and for such and the same ends intents and purposes as I am now or at the time of my decease shall or may be seized of the same hereditaments and premises.

I give and bequeath to my said sister Jane Dunnington the sum of three thousand pounds.

I give and bequeath to my said Brother Thomas Dunnington the sum of five hundred pounds.

I give and bequeath to my said Brother Joseph Dunnington the like sum of five hundred pounds (which I request he will accept as a mark of my affection and regard and that he will understand my reason for not leaving him a larger sum of money is because he will on my death become entitled to the settled Estates of the late Robert Jefferson Esquire.

I give and bequeath to Mrs Ann North of Liverpool in the said County of Lancaster widow the sum of three hundred pounds.

I give and bequeath to Mary Gore the wife of Thomas Gore of Heaton Novis in the said County of Lancaster Gentleman the sum of three hundred pounds.

I give and bequeath to William Kershaw of Liverpool aforesaid Merchant the sum of five hundred pounds.

I give and bequeath to Elizabeth the wife of John Fletcher of the same place Timber Merchant the sum of five Hundred pound.

I give and bequeath unto my Godson John Fletcher the younger the son of the said John Fletcher the sum of Five hundred pounds to be paid to him on his attaining the age of twenty one, but without any interest in the meantime. But if my said Godson shall die before attaining the age of twenty one then the said legacy sum of Five hundred pounds is to lapse and sink into the residue of my personal estate.

I give and bequeath unto Elizabeth Chadwick the wife of Robert Chadwick of Manchester aforesaid Merchant the sum of three hundred pounds.

I give and bequeath unto Susan Whitehead of Liverpool aforesaid widow the sum of three hundred pounds.

I give and bequeath to Charles Whitehead now or late an officer in the East India Company Military service the sum of five hundred pounds.

I give and bequeath to Elizabeth Dunnington (widow of the late Thomas Dunnington of the City of London deceased) the sum of two hundred pounds.

All of which said several legacies or sums of money hereinbefore, respectively given and bequeathed I direct shall be paid by my Executor hereinafter named out of my personal estate within twelve Calendar months next after my decease but without any interest thereon in the meantime And as to for and concerning all the residue and remainder of my personal estate, and effects whatsoever and wheresoever and of what nature or kind soever the same may be after payment thereout of all my just debts funeral expenses the before mentioned legacies and the charges of proving this my Will I direct the same to be divided into two equal moieties or parts.

And one of such equal moieties or parts I give and bequeath unto my said nephew Joseph Dunnington the younger to and for his own use and benefit absolutely for ever.

And as to the other moiety or part of the residue of my said personal estate I give and bequeath the came to my said nephew John his executors administrators and assigns to and for his and their own use and benefit absolutely for ever.

And whereas Robert Jefferson late of Howden in the said County of York esquire deceased in and by his last Will and Testament in writing bearing date on or about the fifteenth day of January one thousand eight hundred and three and by certain codicils thereto or some or one of them gave devised and bequeathed all his Real and personal estate to myself and certain other Trustees for certain purposes therein particularly mentioned And the said Testator thereby directed that certain parts of his said real and personal estates should be sold and converted into money for the purpose of paying off his debts and various annuities legacies and sums of money in and by his said Will and Codicils or some of them mentioned and directed to be paid And whereas in consequence of it being considered advisable and more beneficial for the Estate of the said Robert Jefferson, deceased to postpone the sale of certain parts of the hereditaments in and by his said Will mentioned and directed to be sold for the purposes aforesaid no sale has yet been made or taken place of the whole of such last mentioned hereditaments but I the said John Dunnington Jefferson as the surviving executor of the said Robert Jefferson deceased have from time to time lent and advanced various sums of my own monies for the purpose of paying off and discharging the said several debts annuities legacies and sums of money given and bequeathed or directed to be paid by the said Will and Codicils of the said Robert Jefferson deceased and the same to a considerable amount are still due and owing to me from the Estate of the paid Robert Jefferson Now I hereby direct that when and so soon as the said several sums of money so due and owing to me from the Estate of the said Robert Jefferson or any of them phall be received and gotten in the same shall be added to and form part of the residue of my personal estate and be paid applied and disposed of as in hereinbefore mentioned and directed with respect to my said personal estate provided always and it is my will and mind and direct that my Executor hereby appointed shall be charged and chargeable only for much money as he shall actually receive by virtue of the trusts hereby reposed in him And that he shall not be answerable or accountable for any Bankers Brokers or any other person with whom or in whose hands any part of the said trusts monies shall or may be lodged or deposited for safe custody or otherwise in the execution of the trusts hereinbefore declared And that he shall not be answerable or accountable for the rise or fall in the price or value of the stocks nor for the insufficiency or deficiency in title or value of any security or securities in or from which any part of my personal estate shall be laid out or invested nor for any other misfortune loss or damage which may happen in the execution of this my Will or in relation thereto except the same shall happen by or through his own wilful default respectively and that my said Executor and his executors administrators and assigns shall and may by and out of the money which shall come to his or their respective hands by virtue of this my Will deduct retain to and reimburse to and for himself and themselves respectively all such costs charges damages and expenses and fees to Counsel for advice together with a reasonable allowance for his time and trouble which he they on any of them shall or may suffer sustain expend disburse lay out be at or be put in or about the execution of this my Will or in relation thereto

And lastly I do hereby nominate constitute and appoint my said Brother Thomas Dunnington sole Executor in trust of this my last Will and Testament hereby revoking and making void all former Wills by me at any time heretofore made.

In Witness whereof I the said John Dunnington Jefferson have to this my last Will and Testament contained on seven sheets of paper set my hand this Second day of August in the year of our Lord one thousand eight hundred and thirty four.

Jn° D. Jefferson.

Signed published and declared by the said Testator John Dunnington Jefferson as and for his last Will and Testament in the presence of us who in his presence at his request and in the presence of each other have hereunto subscribed our names as Witnesses R. H Wilson Sol^t Manchester, W. Gregory, E. Halliwell clerks to Mr. Wilson

Codicil

This is a Codicil to be annexed to and taken as part of the last Will and Testament of me John Dunnington Jefferson of Thorganby Hall in the County of Yok Esquire.

Whereas I the said John Dunnington Jefferson have made and duly executed my last Will and Testament in writing dated the second day of August 1834 and thereby amongst other things given and devised certain parts of my Real estates therein particularly mentioned or reserved to unto my nephew John Dunnington his heirs and assigns for ever.

And I have also given and bequeathed unto my said nephew a moiety or equal half part of the residue of my estate and effects for his own use and benefit And whereas since the date and execution of my said will I have purchased divers other Freehold Estates which have already been or are intended to be conveyed unto or in trust for me my heirs and assigns for ever.

And whereas my said nephew John Dunnington has lately died intestate and without issue Now I hereby give and devise unto my only surviving nephew the Reverend Joseph Dunnington of Thicket Hall in the said County of York all and every the several Messuages lands tenements and hereditaments which in and by my said recited Will are given and devised or meant and intended to be given and devised by me unto or for the use and benefit of my said late nephew John Dunnington together with all the rights members and appurtenances thereto respectively belonging To hold all the said several Messuages lands and hereditaments unto and to the use of my said nephew Joseph Dunnington his heirs and assigns for ever.

And I also give and bequeath unto my said nephew Joseph Dunnington all the moiety part and share of my said personal estate and effects which in and by my said will are given and bequeathed by me unto my said late nephew John Dunnington all and every the Messuages lands and hereditaments of every description which I have purchased (and whether already conveyed to me or not) since the date and execution of my said Will To hold the same last mentioned hereditaments and premises unto and to the use of my said nephew Joseph Dunnington his heirs and assigns for ever.

And I hereby confirm my said Will in all other respects save and except as to the two legacies or sums of £500 each thereby given and bequeathed to my brother Joseph and to Charles Whitehead late an Officer in the East India Company service both of which said legacies have lapsed by the deaths of my said Brother and of the said Charles Whitehead.

In Witness whereof I the said John Dunnington Jefferson have hereto set my hand this Sixth of June 1838.

Jnº D. Jefferson

Signed published and declared by the said Testator as and for a Codicil to be annexed to and taken as a part of his will this 6th of June 1838 in the presence of us who in his presence at his request and in the presence of each other have subscribed our names and as witnesses. R. H. Wilson solicitor, Manchester, Thomas Elsworths servant to Mr. Jefferson.

Passed 16 Dec 1840

The Will of Jane Dunnington, 1863
Will ordered through the GOV.UK Find a Will Service[149]

On the seventeenth day of September 1863, the Will of Jane Dunnington of Thorganby Hall in the East Riding of the County of York, Spinster, deceased, who died on the twenty second day of March 1863, at Thorganby Hall aforesaid was proved in the District Registry attached to Her Majesty's Court of Probate at York by the Oath of The Reverend Joseph Dunnington Jefferson of Thicket Priory in the said East Riding of the County of York Clerk the Nephew of the said deceased the sole Executor therein named he having first been sworn to administer.

This is the last Will and Testament of me Jane Dunnington of Thorganby Hall in the East Riding of the County of York Spinster made and published this twenty eight day of November in the year of our Lord one thousand eight hundred and forty six. I give and bequeath to Anna Mervynia the wife of my Nephew The Reverend Joseph Dunnington Jefferson of Thicket Priory in the said East Riding Clerk all my cloathes and wearing apparel to be used and disposed of as she may think proper together with the legacy or sum of nineteen Guineas for the purchase of a mourning ring or other memorial in rembrance of me.

I give devise and bequeath all and every my freehold and copyhold messuages tenements or dwellinghouses closes pieces or parcels of land or ground and hereditaments situate at Kilham, Monk Fryston and Lumby in the West Riding of the said County of York or elsewhere and also all my monies and securities for money and all other my real and personal estate and effects whatsoever and wheresoever and of what nature kind or quality soever and not hereinbefore otherwise disposed of unto my said Nephew Joseph Dunnington Jefferson his heirs executors administrators and assigns to and for his and their own absolute use and benefit but subject to and charged and chargeable with the payments of all my just debts and funeral and testamentary expenses and of the following legacies or sums of money that is to say −

---

[149] https://probatesearch.service.gov.uk/#wills

To my brother Thomas Dunnington with whom I now reside the sum of three hundred pounds

To each of my friends Eliza the wife of John Fletcher of Saint Michael Mount Liverpool in the County of Lancaster Merchant, Elizabeth the wife of Robert Chadwick of Oakfield Salford in the said County of Lancaster Merchant, Jane Bell of Reedness Street ?asholme in the City of York widow, Elizabeth the wife of The Reverend [blank] Greenstreet now residing in the South of England and daughter of the said John and Elizabeth Fletcher, and Elizabeth Christiana the widow of my late Nephew John Dunnington now residing at Middlewood Hall in the said West Riding the sum of one hundred pounds

To each of my said brother's two servants Mary Etherington and Thomas Elsworth provided they shall be living with us at the time of my decease the sum of nineteen Guineas

And to my said brother's other servant Ann Makin provided she also be living with us the sum of ten guineas

All which said legacy of three hundred pounds five several sums of one hundred pounds each two several sums of nineteen guineas and said sum of ten guineas I do hereby give and bequeath to my said brother, Eliza Fletcher, Elizabeth Chadwick, Jane Bell, Eliza Jane Greenstreet, Elizabeth Christiana Dunnington, Mary Etherington, Thomas Elsworth, and Ann Makin respectively accordingly and direct the same to be paid to them respectively by my said Nephew within twelve calendar months after my decease

And I give and devise all mortgage and trust estates which may at the time of my decease be vested in me or any person or persons in trust for me unto my said Nephew Joseph Dunnington Jefferson his heirs executors administrators and assigns subject to the equities and trusts affecting the same in order that he of they may be enabled to convey and transfer the same without it being necessary to have recourse to my Heir at Law or any other person to join therein

And lastly I do hereby nominate constitute and appoint my said Nephew Joseph Dunnington Jefferson sole Executor of this my Will and do hereby revoke all former and other Will and Wills by me at any time heretofore made and do declare this and this only to be my last Will and Testament

In witness whereof I the said Jane Dunnington the Testatrix have hereunto set my hand and seal the day and year first before written –

Jane Dunnington [initialled] Jane Dunnington [signed in full]

Signed and published and declared by the said Jane Dunnington the Testatrix as and for her last Will and Testament in the presence of us who in her presence at her request and in the presence of each other have subscribed our names as Witness therto

J. B. Burland, solt. South Cave
Thomas Strickland

In Her Majesty's Court of Probate The District Registry at York In the goods of Jane Dunnington deceased I Joseph Blanchard Burland of South Cave in the County of York Gentleman make oath that I am one of the subscribing witnesses to the last Will and Testament of Jane Dunnington late of Thorganby Hall in the East Riding of the County of York Spinster deceased the said Will being now hereunto annexed bearing date the twenty eight day of November one thousand eight hundred and forty six And having now carefully perused the said Will and observed two signatures of the said deceased at the foot or end thereof as follows "Jane Dunnington" "Jane Dunnington" the said last signature being written underneath the said first mentioned signature I further make Oath and say that the said deceased who was then in a very weak state of health first wrote the first mentioned signature but the same not being considered sufficiently clear the deceased thereupon again signed her name to wit the said last mentioned signature in manner as now appears that theron And I lastly make Oath that the said deceased made both to said signatures at the foot or end of the said Will at the same time on the day of the date thereof in the presence of me and of Thomas Strickland the other subscribed Witness thereto both of us being present at the same time and we thereupon attested and subscribed said Will in the presence of the said Testatrix
J. B. Burland
Sworn at Brantingham in the County of York on the twelfth day of September 1863 Before me – Charles J. Shackles, a Commissioner to administer Oaths in Chancery in England.

In Her Majesty's Court of Probate - York District Registry
On the seventeenth day of September 1863 the Will of Jane Dunnington late
of Thorganby Hall in the East Riding of the County of York Spinster deceased
was proved by the oath of The Reverend Joseph Dunnington Jefferson Clerk
the Nephew of the said deceased the sole Executor named in the said Will he
having been first sworn duly to administer.

Effects under £1,000
Probate extracted by Burland & Son, Solicitors South Cave This is a true
copy.

The Will of Rev. Joseph Dunnington-Jefferson, 1880
Will ordered through the GOV.UK Find a Will Service

The will of the Reverend Joseph Dunnington Jefferson, late of Thicket Priory, clerk, Canon of York, who died 31 July 1880 at Ticehurst, Sussex.

My dear wife Anna Mervynia Dunnington Jefferson to have free use, but not the right of disposal, of my mansion house called Thicket Priory, and of the park, gardens, pleasure grounds, coach houses, stables, plate, linen, china, glass, books, pictures, prints, furniture, wines, stores, horses, carriages, cows, poultry, pigs and household goods, in my house and grounds at the time of my death, for one year.

And that during that year all parliamentary and other taxes, rates, charges and assessments and other outgoings payable shall be paid out of my general personal estate.

I bequeath to my said dear wife one carriage and a pair of carriage horses with harness as she may select for her own use and benefit.

I devise all my lands tenements, hereditaments, and real estates in the East and West Ridings of York or elsewhere and being freehold or copyhold or customaryhold, (except the building ground at Hook and Goole, and what I otherwise dispose of in this my will or codicil, for the use of my wife for one year from my death) to the use of my eldest son Joseph John Dunnington Jefferson and Thomas Blanchard Burland of South Cave for two years from my death, without impeachment of waste. But if I should die at a period more than five years after the date of this my will then for the alternative term of one year only from my death.

Upon the trusts hereinafter declared. As to my mansion house of Thicket Priory and my estate lands, tenements etc. situated in Thorganby cum Cottingwith, Wheldrake, East Cottingwith, Duffield, Skipwith, North Newbald and Barlby in the East Riding, and at Hook in the West Riding (except certain building land in Hook near Goole, herineafter devised upon certain trusts for sale in manner hereinafter mentioned) I give and devise the same to the use and intent that my wife may receive during her widowhood the yearly rent-charge of one thousand pounds charged upon the said premises, by equal payments on the 24 June and 25 December in every year after the expiration of the two years or the alternative term of one year hereinbefore limited, with right of entry and distress in case of default after 21 days.

And I declare that subject to these charges the said heridaments and premises shall remain and be to the use of my said eldest son Joseph John Dunnington Jefferson, for his life, and after his decease to the use of the first and every other son of the said Joseph John Dunnington Jefferson, according to their respective seniorities, and in default of such issue to the use of my second son, Mervyn Dunnington Jefferson for his life, after his decease to the use of the first and every other son of the said Mervyn Dunnington Jefferson, according to their respective seniorities, and in default of such issue to the use of my third son, Thomas Trafford Dunnington Jefferson for his life, after his decease to the use of the first and every other son of the said Thomas Trafford Dunnington Jefferson, according to their respective seniorities, in tail, provided also and I declare to be legal, for any of my said sons to appoint a woman they may marry to have such tenancy for her life, all subject to the same annual rent-charge of one thousand pounds to my wife.

And as to my estates lands and hereditaments in the parishes of Howden, Barmby on the Marsh, Skelton, and other townships now or heretofore in the parish of Howden, and the parishes or townships of Selby, Brayton, Thorp Willoughby, Hambleton, Hillam and Monk Fryston in the West Riding, I give and devise the same, subject to the said term of two years or alternative term of one year and to the trusts thereof hereinafter declared, unto and to the use of my second son the said Mervyn Dunnington Jefferson, and after his decease to the use of the first and every other son of the said Mervyn Dunnington Jefferson, according to their respective seniorities in tail, and in default of such issue to the use of my eldest son the said Joseph John Dunnington Jefferson for his life, and after his decease to the use of the first and every other son successively in tail.

And as to the residue and remainder of these lands in Howden etc. in case of default or failure of such issue, unto the use of my third son, Thomas Trafford Dunnington Jefferson for his life, after his decease to the use of the first and every other son of the said Thomas Trafford Dunnington Jefferson, according to their respective seniorities, in tail.

And as to my estates lands and hereditaments in the parishes or townships of Bubwith, Harlethorpe, Eastrington, Bellasize, Newport, Gilberdike and other townships (except Howden) in the neighbourhood of Eastrington, I give and devise the same, subject to the said term of two years or alternative term of one year and to the trusts thereof hereinafter declared, unto and to the use of my third son the said Thomas Trafford Dunnington Jefferson and after his decease to the use of the first and every other son successively in tail of the said Mervyn Dunnington Jefferson, according to their respective seniorities in tail in like manner.

And as to the residue and remainder of these lands in Bubwith etc. in case of default or failure of such issue of my sons Mervyn and Thomas Trafford, unto the use of my eldest son, Joseph John Dunnington Jefferson for his life, and after his decease to the use of the first and every other son of the said Joseph Dunnington Jefferson, according to their respective seniorities, in tail, in like manner.

And my trustees to pay the following sums:

To my said wife the annual sum of one thousand pounds

To my eldest son Joseph John Dunnington Jefferson, the annual sum of one thousand pounds

To each of my sons, Mervyn and Thomas Trafford four hundred pounds annually

Building plots in Goole and Hook to the use of my eldest son Joseph John Dunnington Jefferson and Thomas Blanchard Burland to sell or lease as they see fit, provided, that they keep in repair all the other lands and premises and improve where necessary.

I give and bequeath to my said wife, one thousand pounds, one year after my death, and all her jewels trinkets and personal ornaments.

I give and bequeath to my eldest son Joseph John Dunnington Jefferson all my plate linen china glass books pictures prints furniture wines stores (less those consumed) and household goods whatsoever after one year from my death or after the death of my wife.

I bequeath all the money securities for money, goods, redits and personal estate unto the said Joseph John Dunnington Jefferson and Thomas Blanchard Burland, upon trust, pay my funeral expenses, testamentary expenses debts and legacies, and out of the residue set apart three sums of fifteen thousand pounds to my three daughters, Mervynia Jane Dunnington Jefferson, Mary Campbell Dunnington Jefferson, and Theodosia Dunnington Jefferson, and place the sums in public stocks or other investments and pay the dividends to my daughters during her life, independent of any husband, to provide for their maintenance and education.

If they die with no issue, then defaults to my three sons. All residue to my eldest son Joseph John Dunnington Jefferson.

I hereby appoint my eldest son Joseph John Dunnington Jefferson and my friend Thomas Blanchard Burland exectors of this my last will and guardians together with my wife of my infant children during their minorities.

In witness whereof I have set my hand seal the 30th October 1867. J. D Jefferson

Witnesses:

J. B. Burland, solicitor of South Cave, and Richard Petch, his clerk.

Admon of Thomas Trafford Dunnington-Jefferson Esq., 1882
Will ordered through the GOV.UK Find a Will Service

(1st Grant)
18 October 1882.
Administration of the Personal Estate of Thomas Trafford Dunnington-Jefferson late of Thicket Priory in the East Riding of the County of York Esquire, a Bachelor who died 1 April 1882 at the "Midland" Hotel in the County of Middlesex was granted at the Principal Registry to Joseph John Dunnington-Jefferson of Thicket Priory Esquire the Brother.
Personal Estate £1,357 12s. 8d.

(2nd Grant)
12 August 1942.
Dunnington-Jefferson
Thomas Trafford of Thicket Priory Thorganby Yorkshire died 1 April 1882 at The Midland Hotel Middlesex Administration Llandudno 12 August to John Alexander Dunnington-Jefferson D.S.O. retired lieutenant-colonel H.M. army.
Effects £2,424 12s.
Former Grant P.R. 18 October 1882.

The Will of Anna Mervynia Dunnington-Jefferson, 1898
Will ordered through the GOV.UK Find a Will Service

Be it known, that at the date hereunder written, the last Will and Testament with a codicil thereto of Anna Mervyn Dunnington Jefferson of Durrants Hotel Manchester Square in the County of Middlesex, Widow formerly of Scarborough in the County of York and of No. 14 Westover Villas Bournemouth in the County of Southampton, deceased, who died on the 2nd day of November 1898, at Durrants Hotel aforesaid

was proved and registered in the Principal Probate Registry of His Majesty's High Court of Justice, and that administration of all the estate which by law devolves to and vests in the personal representative of the said deceased was granted by the aforesaid Court to Joseph John Dunnington Jefferson of Thicket Priory in the said County of York Esquire the son the executor named in the said Will and Mervyn Dunnington Jefferson of Middlethorpe Hall York in the said County of York Esquire the son also and Theodosia Dunnington Jefferson of Durrants Hotel aforesaid Spinster the daughter the executors named in the said Codicil.

Dated 5th day of December 1898

Gross value of Estate £4723 14s
Net Value of Personal Estate £4634 7s. 7d.

THIS IS THE LAST WILL AND TESTAMENT

of me ANNA MERVYNIA DUNNINGTON JEFFERSON now at Scarborough in the County of York widow made and published this twentieth day of July in the year of our Lord One thousand and eight hundred and eighty two I appoint my eldest son Joseph John Dunnington Jefferson SOLE EXECUTOR of this my Will I bequeath the following legacies namely the sum of one hundred pounds to my said son Joseph John Dunnington Jefferson The sum of one hundred pounds to my son Mervyn Dunnington Jefferson the sum of one hundred pounds to my daughter Mary Campbell the wife of William Robert White the sum of one twenty five pounds to my friend Thomas Blanchard Burland of South Cave in the said County of York Solicitor The sum of twenty five pounds to my friend Charles Isherwood

Burland of Shanklin in the Isle of Wight Clerk in Holy Orders The sum of twenty five pounds to the Church of England Missionary Society And the sum of twenty five pounds to the London Society for the Propagation of Christianity amongst the Jews And I direct that the said Charitable Legacies be paid exclusively out of such part of my personal estate as may lawfully be appropriated to such purposes and in preference to any other payment thereout and that the receipt of the Treasurer for the time being of the said Societies respectively shall be a sufficient discharge to my executor for the said Charitable legacies respectively And that all the above several legacies shall be paid free from legacy duty within twelve calendar months after my decease I give and devise and bequeath all the rest residue and remainder of my real and personal estate whatsoever and wheresoever and whther in possession reversion remainder or expectancy of or to or over which I shall at my death be seized possessed or entitled or have any power of disposition by Will subject to the payment thereout of my just debts funeral and testamentary expenses and as to estates vested in me as trustee or mortgagee subject to the trusts and equities afecting the same respectively Unto and equally between my two daughters Mervynia Jane Dunnington Jefferson and Theodosia Dunnington Jefferson their respective heirs executors administrators and assigns absolutely share and share alike as tenants in common but I request them to present to my brother Sir Henry Mervyn Vavasour and also to my sister Emma Matilda Dod some of my books or some other of my trinkets to keep in remembrance of me I direct that all monies estates and interests devolving upon or accruing to any woman under this my Will shall be held and enjoyed by her as and for her own sole use and separate use and benefit absolutely free from maritaal control And lastly I hereby revoke all other Wills IN WITNESS whereof I the said Anna Mervynia Dunnington Jefferson the testratrix have hereunto set my hand and seal the day and year first before written - ANNA MERVYNIA DUNNINGTON JEFFERSON (LS) Signed sealed published and declared by the said Anna Mervynia Dunnington Jefferson the Testatrix as and for her last Will and Testament in the presence of us present at the same time who at her request in her presence and in the presence of each other have hereunto subscribed our names as witnesses – FRANCIS WILLIAM JAMES SEWELL Lieut Colonel Scarborough. – M D'ARCY WYVILL Richmond Yorkshire

I ANNA MERVYNIA DUNNINGTON JEFFERSON
Formerly of Scarborough in the County of York but now temporarily residing
at 14 Westover Villas Bourmemouth in the County of Hants Widow declare
this to be a codicil to my last Will which bears date the twentieth day of July
One thousand and eight hundred and eighty two I appoint my son Captain
Mervyn Dunnington Jefferson and my daughter Theodosia Dunnington
Jefferson to be EXECUTOR AND EXECUTRIX AND TRUSTEES of my
said Will to act jointly with my son Joseph John Dunnington Jefferson who is
thereby appointed sole executor and trustee And I declare that my said Will
shall be construed and take effect in all respects as if the names of the said
Mervyn Dunnington Jefferson and Theodosia Dunnington Jefferson had been
originally inserted therein throughout in addition to the name of the said
Joseph John Dunnington Jefferson as the executors and trustees of thereof
And in all other respects I confirm my said Will IN WITNESS whereof I the
said Anna Mervynia Dunnington Jefferson the Testatrix have to this Codicil to
my last Will set my hand this second day of June One thousand eight hundred
and ninety seven –
ANNA MERVYNIA DUNNINGTON JEFFERSON – Signed and declared by
the above named Anna Mervynia Dunnington Jefferson the Testatrix as and
for a Codicil to her last Will in the presence of us present at the same time
who in her presence at her request and in the presence of each other have
hereunto subscribed our names as witnesses the word "Jefferson" being
interlined prior to execution – WILLIAM FAZER Elmhurst Bournemouth
M.D. – SARAH ELIZA YEO 14 Westover Villas Bourmemouth Lodging
House Keeper.

On the 5th day of December 1898 Probate of this Will with a Codicil was
granted to Joseph John Dunnington Jefferson Mervyn Dunnington Jefferson
and Theodosia Dunnington Jefferson the Executors.